The Economic Prerequisite
to Democracy

D0733050

For Ann and David

DAN USHER

The Economic Prerequisite
to Democracy

New York · Columbia University Press

Printed in the United States of America.

Library of Congress Cataloging in Publication Data

Usher, Dan, 1934 —
    The economic prerequisite to democracy

    Includes bibliographical references and index.
    1. Economics. 2. Democracy — Economic aspects.
    3. Right of property. 4. Income distribution.
    5. Economic policy. I. Title.
    HB73.U84   330.12'2   81—1430
    ISBN 0–231–05281–2   AACR2

Contents

Preface

The legislature, were it possible that its deliberations could be always directed, not by the clamorous importunity of partial interests, but by an extensive view of the general good, ought upon this very account, perhaps, to be particularly careful neither to establish any new monopolies of this kind, nor to extend further those which are already established. Every such regulation introduces some degree of real disorder into the constitution of the state, which it will be difficult afterwards to cure without occasioning another disorder.

Adam Smith[1]

One way or another, every society must decide who is to be rich and who is to be poor, who is to command and who is to be commanded, who is to occupy posts generally considered desirable and who is to occupy posts generally considered undesirable. Every society is confronted with the task of what we shall call *assignment*, though different societies deal with it in different ways. In some societies the remunerative, prestigious, power-wielding or interesting posts are hereditary. In others they are open to competition in physical strength or educational attainment. In still others they may be dependent on ownership of property. Assignment may be the outcome of a collective decision, of a great many decisions citizens make for themselves, of custom, or, as is usually the case, of a combination of these. Desirable characteristics of situations — income, power and intrinsic interest — frequently come together, but they may do so to a greater or lesser extent, as in the contrast between a feudal society where it is absolutely clear who is on the bottom and who is on top and a modern industrial society where, on occasion, leading politicians live modestly, rich men have very little power, and scientists or artists who think of their jobs as the most exciting in the world have neither power, in the normal sense of the word, nor money to speak of. Conflict over assignment may conceivably be eliminated in primitive tribes where property is equally divided or collective and where hierarchy is unnecessary, but there is no such possibility in an advanced industrial society where hierarchy, property or both are an absolute requirement.

Conflict over assignment is especially troublesome in democratic societies for reasons that have been recognized from the very beginning of political theory in ancient Greece. There is, on the one hand, a contradiction between the basic, rock-bottom equality of citizens as voters and the necessary inequality of citizens as property-owners or as members of industrial or political hierarchies to which people must somehow be assigned. Inequality is accommodated easily enough in a monarchy or one-party state where no institution exists by which those of low income or status may force a change of place with their betters. In a democracy, however, the leadership may be overthrown, the powerful deprived of their sources of power and the rich dispossessed by a simple vote of the legislature. There is, on the other hand, an intrinsic instability to democracy. The principle of majority rule allows any coalition of 51 per cent of the legislature to have its way over the remaining 49 per cent. It follows immediately that no one can be secure with the income and status that society has assigned to him because every assignment can be overturned by a coalition of voters determined to appropriate the highest incomes and the choice positions in the hierarchy for its members. Recognition of these difficulties has made men hesitant to adopt a democratic form of government, and still gives one cause to wonder why democratic government works in many countries. Why is the vote not more frequently directed against the unpopular, the rich and those unfortunate enough to find themselves in linguistic, religious or geographic minorities? Why, understanding this possibility, are citizens prepared to subject themselves to the rules of democracy? Why, once established, does democracy not lead to such a game of musical chairs, of coalitions in the legislature displacing other coalitions interminably, with people's incomes and status rising or falling at the whim of the electorate, that there develops a mutual agreement among citizens to replace democracy with some more authoritarian form of government? To be sure, democracies have collapsed through failure to deal adequately with the assignment of income and other advantages; but not all democracies have failed, and it is of the greatest importance to understand how successful democracies have been preserved.

The contradiction between the rules of democratic government and the necessity of assignment in a modern industrial society can be resolved in only one way. If the legislature cannot handle the assignment of income, desirable occupations and positions of authority, then another means must be found to do the job. For democracy to survive, there must be a prior agreement among citizens on a set of rules for assignment that voters or legislators will not lightly overturn. We shall refer to this as a *system of equity*, defined as 'a set of rules for assigning income and other advantages independently of and prior to political decisions arrived at in the legislature'. Clearly, the rules cannot be all-encompassing. Political leaders have to be chosen by vote, and their incomes and status must inevitably rise or fall according to the will of the electorate. Everything the legislature does in domestic and even in foreign affairs must have consequences for the relative incomes and status of citizens. But there is a difference between a society where the great majority of people are confident that their income and status depend primarily on non-political factors, inherited wealth, luck or their own ability, and a society where citizens rightly attribute their rise or decline to their success in mustering a political party or pressure group to act on their behalf. A complete and perfect system of equity would need to be so comprehensive that it would leave the legislature with nothing whatsoever to do. An adequate system, which is all we really care about, is one that leaves a large enough share of the typical man's income to be determined outside of and independently of the political arena, limiting what he has to gain if the voting goes his way and what he has to lose if it does not, that he is prepared to live within the rules of democracy and is not tempted by a more authoritarian form of government.

The legislature is always able to choose an assignment of income, but it is not always able to desist from choosing. Society may be so organized that there is a prior, recognized and established assignment which the legislature may leave undiscussed and unaltered, or only slightly modified, from year to year. The economy may generate an assignment of income or there may be a well-established tradition as to who has the right to what. If in addition there is no majority with an incentive to overturn the established assignment and to replace it with another, we say that there is a system of equity. But there may be no such privileged assignment. The economy may produce goods without at the same time yielding a socially-recognized prescription as to who is to receive the goods, so that the legislature is forced to assign income and status whether it would wish to do so or not. In that case we say that there is no system of equity. Which of these alternatives is realized, or – to be more precise – where on the continuum between the poles of political assignment and non-political assignment a particular country lies, depends in large measure on how the economy is organized.

This book is a study of how society protects democratic government by entrusting the economy with the task that the legislature can never perform – the task of assigning the major part of income and other advantages. Not all forms of economic organization are capable of performing this task, and none performs it perfectly. It is, therefore, possible to evaluate policies and forms of economic organization according to their compatibility with democratic govenment. The normal procedure in economic analysis – in cost-benefit analysis, in public finance, in trade policy and so on – is to rank options on a criterion of efficiency (where the more efficient option is that conducive to the larger national income), modified, perhaps, for effects on equality in the income distribution or for aspects of welfare not adequately represented by national income as conventionally defined. I am proposing a radically different criterion. I argue that it is possible to consider the choice between capitalism, socialism and other forms of economic organization and to analyse a wide range of policy issues – the redistribution of income, socialized medicine, anti-trust policy, the public subsidization of investment by private firms, tax policy, and the choice of the agenda for the public sector – not from the point of view of efficiency, but according to whether the system of equity is strengthened or attenuated; whether democratic government is made more or less secure.

The issues in each case are whether the particular form of economic organization increases or reduces the extent to which income and other advantages have to be assigned within the legislature and whether the method of assignment prior to the political process is rendered more or less tolerable to a majority of voters. These are not, unfortunately, matters about which we can reason with even the limited precision that ordinary economic analysis has attained. The analysis is fuzzy at the edges, and less rigorous as we go from step to step than I would like it to be. There is, in addition, a complicated intermingling of our new political criterion and the traditional criteria of efficiency and equality. Nonetheless, I believe it important to introduce the political criterion because there is a connection between economic organization and political life, and because we may make serious errors of judgement if the political criterion is ignored.

Throughout the book, we find ourselves dealing with matters normally thought of as belonging to the domain of political belief rather than to the domain of what can be evaluated in a systematic and dispassionate way. It is arguable that one favours socialism or capitalism just as one is Christian or Muslim, and that the merits of the two systems cannot be analysed in the spirit in which one would analyse the relative merits of alternative tax structures. There is some truth to the argument, as a description of the psychology of adherents and because choices among alternative forms of economic organization must ultimately depend on one's values. If people agree in their assessments of what life would be like under socialism and under capitalism, and if they still disagree about which is preferable – some favouring the society that would emerge under capitalism, and others favouring the society that would emerge under socialism – then we are indeed up against a barrier we cannot cross, unless, of course, one or both parties can be persuaded that its assessment is mistaken. But I do not think that people agree about the facts, and I suspect that disagreement is particularly strong over the political implications of economic organization, precisely because these have not been examined systematically. In so far as the consequences of alternative forms of economic organization are at issue, and not the desirability of the consequences, then the choice among systems depends more on facts than on values, and does become amenable to the kind of analysis one might apply in considering alternative tax structures or foreign trade regimes. That the criterion is the preservation of democracy rather than the maximization of the national income requires a change in the way the problem is handled, but does not make the problem any less fitting a subject for rigorous analysis and does not justify a stance in which the problem cannot be touched because it belongs to the domain of opinion and belief. The provisional value throughout the book will be the preservation of democracy; economic policy will be analysed with respect to that criterion alone, in the first instance, and together with efficiency and equality later on.

This book should be easily read by anyone with a minimal acquaintance with economic ideas, as long as one potential stumbling block can be put out of the way. The reader must recognize that I coin two technical terms, *assignment* and *equity*, and that I use the word *political* in a somewhat unusual sense. Wherever these words appear, they must be understood precisely as defined, and some of their normal connotations must be put aside.

When a new concept is to be introduced and a name chosen by which it may be referred, an author can take one of two routes. He can invent an entirely new word, as is the practice when an organism is first named in biology; or he can redefine a word in common use, as tends to be the practice in the social sciences. The advantage of the first procedure is clarity; the advantage of the second is that some of the original connotations of the word fit the new concept, and the overlap between old and new meanings is an aid to understanding how the new concept is being employed. New and old meanings of the word must be reasonably close for this advantage to obtain, but they cannot be identical if there is to be a new concept at all. Virtually all of the technical terms in economics – 'demand', 'supply', 'rent', 'profit', 'capital', 'utility' – have their origin in common speech, and are used within economics in ways that are similar, but not identical, to their usages outside. So, too, with the usages of the terms 'assignment', 'political' and 'equity' in this book.

Of the three terms, the term 'assignment' is used in a sense closest to the ordinary usage of the word, and is the least likely to give rise to confusion. It refers here to whatever process society employs to differentiate among people, with emphasis on circumstances where equality is either too costly or not feasible at all and where a means must be found to decide who shall be favoured and who shall not. Assignment of people to slots in a hierarchy is where our usage and the common usage are most nearly in accord. We shall also speak of the assignment of property through the institution of inheritance, and of the assignment of incomes to people through whatever process society employs to decide who is to be rich and who is to be poor. The words 'allocation' or 'apportionment' might have been used instead, for they do carry many of the right connotations. I preferred not to use 'allocation' because it is too closely tied to the concept of property and because it carries the connotation in economics of allocating factors to the production of goods rather than of allocating goods to people. I preferred not to use 'apportionment' because, though it has the right connotations with respect to dividing up income, it does not carry over well to the placing of people in jobs. All three words have a more activist connotation than I would prefer. To speak of assignment suggests that there is someone who assigns, while I want to include processes, such as one finds in markets, with no central decision-making at all.

The meaning of 'assignment' is narrowed considerably when we speak of reassignment as contrasted with redistribution. As will be discussed in detail, the distinction is between a reordering of people on a scale (the president and vice-president change jobs), and a narrowing of the income distribution. It is, in fact, the close association of the term 're-distribution' with the promotion of equality – an association I want to preserve – that led me to avoid using the word 'distribution' to denote what I use the word 'assignment' to mean.

Our usage of the word 'political' is again quite close to common speech, but there is an important distinction to bear in mind. Normally, when one speaks of a political criterion for the evaluation of economic policy, one has in mind a constraint that voters or politicians have imposed. An economist or a technician may say that such-and-such policy is advisable on some criterion, but is politically impossible. That is not the sense of the word 'political' in the context of this book. Here, the political criterion is almost technological. It refers to the impact of economic policy on government, specifically of the effects upon the viability of democratic government, regardless of whether the policy is politically acceptable in the common meaning of the term. Thus, we may say that there is a political case to be made for (or against) socialized medicine on the grounds that democratic government is likely to work better (or worse) when medicine is socialized than when it is private. An economy with socialized medicine may be politically advantageous, in our sense of the word 'political', because the legislature is absolved from having to make certain kinds of decisions that affect the assignment of income or because it provides an extra incentive for citizens to uphold the system of equity in force. Socialized medicine could be politically advantageous in this sense though neither politicians nor citizens favour it, or it could be politically disadvantageous despite universal support. Whether socialized medicine really is politically advantageous in this sense is discussed in the last chapter of the book. What needs emphasis here is that the political criterion is different from efficiency and from the question of what citizens or legislators are inclined to support.

The word *equity* is the real problem. Recall that a *system of equity* is defined as 'a set of rules for assigning income and other advantages to citizens independently of and prior to political decisions arrived at in the legislature'. 'Equity' in this book refers to any non-political means of assignment that society employs, where 'non-political' is meaningful only in the context of a democratic society. A means of assignment is non-political in this sense as long as the assignment is not chosen by voters or by the legislature. The election of a president cannot be a part of any system of equity. The determination of who shall be rich and who shall be poor through the institution of inheritance, or by some procedure having to do with individual skill, strength, intelligence or determination, can be part of a system of equity because, and only because, the legislature need not concern itself with the matter. Even slavery could be part of a system of equity — as it was in ancient Greece — as long as the legislature's role in determining who owns whom is limited to the resolution of minor disputes at the edges of an otherwise well-established set of rules.

Clearly, equity as defined in this book is not the same as justice or equality, but they are related in the sense that justice and equality are attributes that a system of equity may, but need not, possess. A particular system of equity may be characterized as just or unjust, and it may be more or less conducive to equality of income and status among citizens. The distinction between equity and equality needs emphasis because, as will be explained later on, full equality is one among several conceivable systems of equity and because there has developed an unfortunate usage of words in the discipline of economics according to which equity is treated as a synonym for equality. That is not the usage here.

Why have we invented such a concept, and why did we choose a name with so many connotations we wish to avoid? The concept of equity is introduced because, as mentioned briefly above and as will be explained in detail later on, the legislature cannot attend to the assignment of income and other advantages, except to a limited extent, without destroying democracy in the process. The preservation of democracy requires a non-political method of assignment, and it is convenient to have a generic term for all possible sets of arrangements that can do the job. The word 'equity' is chosen because I cannot think of a word that comes closer to what I want equity to mean. The word does, however, have more or less the right connotations when one speaks, for instance, of the equity in one's house or of an equitable settlement of claims to land. In the latter case particularly, the equitable outcome is that in accordance with customary procedures for determining who has title to what; an equal division of land among claimants or a division determined on the basis of a vote in the local legislature (unless the legislature itself feels bound by the system of equity) would not necessarily be equitable in the normal sense of the term or in the technical sense in this book.

The writing of this book has had a curious beginning. Some years ago I did a study of a Canadian programme of subsidies to firms for investing in less developed regions of the country. I came to believe that the programme was harmful on balance, in part because its ultimate beneficiaries were not those the programme was designed to assist, but primarily because of its political consequences. I became convinced for reasons I could not at first articulate that democratic government would be more costly to run and more difficult to maintain if programmes of this kind were allowed to proliferate, though the programme itself was too small to do any real harm. At about the same time I was studying elementary game theory and social choice, and it occurred to me that a standard problem in the dynamics of majority rule − that there is no equilibrium assignment of a given total income among voters in a legislature with majority rule − could at once explain my unease about the programme of investment subsidies and rationalize a great deal of economic organization and policy. My first attempts to develop this idea were in two Queen's Discussion Papers: 'A Critique of the Canadian Program of Subsidizing Investment in Less Developed Regions' (no. 145, 1974) and 'The Problem of Equity' (no. 181, 1975).

In formulating my ideas, I benefited considerably from discussion with colleagues and students, especially John Fountain, Scott Gordon, Walter Hettich, Steve Kaliski, Michael Prime, T.K. Rymes and Klaus Stegemann. The second paper was revised while I was on sabbatical at Nuffield College, Oxford. Comments at that time from Walter Elkin, Michael Freeman, Alan Williams and Jack Wiseman were particularly helpful. The first draft of the present manuscript was completed while I was a visiting Fellow at the Hoover Institution at Stanford. I thank the Director and Fellows of the Hoover Institution for providing me with the leisure and with an excellent environment for completing this work. The present version has incorporated several comments and suggestions that emerged when I presented this material at seminars at Carleton

University, Johns Hopkins, and at the Center for Public Choice at Virginia Polytechnic Institute and State University. Bill Furlong and Arthur Stewart, graduate students at Queen's University, helped with the preparation of the final manuscript.

The geography of the book is accidental. The argument is basically theoretical, just as much of economics is theoretical, in the sense of having no geographic or historic limits. Economic institutions and policies are said to have political consequences regardless of when or where they are to be found. But, as the analysis is somewhat informal and the theoretical model is a considerable simplification of democratic politics, it is helpful to buttress the argument with examples, drawn indiscriminately from Canada, the United States and the United Kingdom, the countries with which I am most familiar and to which the policy prescriptions are most likely to apply.

1

Introduction

. . . the principle of capitalism cannot be squared with the principle of democracy. The one consistently seeks to maintain inequalities which the other, not less consistently, seeks to abolish . . . either democracy must transform capitalism or capitalism must suppress democracy . . . .

Harold J. Laski[1]

It is often said that democracy will not tolerate capitalism. If capitalism means here a competitive system based on free disposal over private property, it is far more important to realize that only within this system is democracy possible. When it becomes dominated by a collectivist creed, democracy will inevitably destroy itself.

Friedrich A. Hayek[2]

Between socialism . . . and democracy there is no necessary relation; the one can exist without the other. At the same time there is no incompatibility; in appropriate states of social environment, the socialist engine can be run on democratic principles.

Joseph A. Schumpeter[3]

Democracy is a precarious form of government. There have only been a few instances of democracy prior to the eighteenth century, and while we look upon the early democracies as societies of great achievement, we must recognize that they were limited to city states and were less durable than other forms of government. In this century many new democracies have been founded, but few have lasted, and most have given way to military dictatorship or the one party state. With perhaps a half dozen exceptions, democratic governments, where they occur, seem to be unstable, tottering with great uncertainty as to whether and how long they can continue. The prospects for the continuance of democratic government may be, as the quotation from Schumpeter would suggest, more or less independent of economic policy. It may be that politics goes on one track and economics goes on another, with little contact between them. If that is so, the economist (or anyone with decisions to make about the formulation of economic policy) need be concerned only about prosperity and equality, taking political insti- tutions as constraints and hoping that whatever causes political develop- ments will permit democratic government to continue. But if that is not so, if there is a direct link from economic policy to democracy, it becomes incumbent upon us to widen our focus and to consider a broader range of consequences than would otherwise be relevant, lest policies designed to increase the efficiency of the economy fail, even on that limited criterion, because they increase the cost of maintaining demo- cratic government or place democratic government in jeopardy.

Despite their differences, Laski and Hayek as quoted above are closer to one another than either is to Schumpeter. Laski and Hayek agree that the economy is not autonomous, that economic policy can affect the political realm, and that the political consequences of economic policy may be as important as their economic consequences. I suspect that the economics profession is schizophrenic on this issue. If asked directly whether economic policy has political consequences, most economists would say that it does. But the practice of economists is, for the most part, though considerably less now than was the case a decade or two ago,[4] to ignore political consequences altogether and to reason as though prosperity and equality were their only concerns.

If we agree in principle that Laski and Hayek are correct in their major premise, we are immediately confronted with the question, not so much of who is right on the issue where they differ, as of how we go about deciding who is right. What theories can guide us in deciding whether socialism or capitalism is the more compatible with democracy? What facts have a bearing on the matter? It is significant that, on my reading of the texts from which the quotations are taken, Laski and Hayek differ less in their values than in their formal analysis of society. A difference in values is at bottom irreconcilable, but a difference in analysis can in principle be resolved through the triumph of one view or by the incor- poration of both views in a greater generalization, more or less as disputes in the sciences are eventually resolved. If I am correct in supposing the difference between Laski and Hayek to be attributable to analysis rather than to values, it should be possible to resolve the issue between them or to identify the elements in the large packages of policies we call socialism and capitalism most conducive to the maintenance of demo- cratic government.

The silence of formal economic theory on the political consequences of economic policy is not accidental. It is attributable to a characteristic of economic theory that has much to do with its success as a tool of analysis in many of the problems economists are called upon to deal with. The basic model of economics is of a self-contained economy where firms maximise profit in deciding what to produce, consumers maximize welfare in deciding how much labour to supply and how to allocate income among the available goods and services, and the initial distribution among citizens of the ownership of resources is accepted as a fact not subject to analysis. The strong model differentiates economics from the other social sciences and lends economics whatever success it may have in such matters as predicting who will lose and who will gain from a change in the tax rates, assessing whether the benefits of roads, airports, or other public projects exceed the costs of the tax required to finance them, and designing policies to promote full employment and economic growth.

The economic model[5] is connected to the political process in one sense, but is completely cut off from it in another. It is connected in the sense that the influence of politics on the economy – through changes in tax rates, expectations or the rules governing economic behaviour – is easily accounted for as changes in parameters of the model. In fact, a good case can be made for the proposition that, as suggested by the older term 'political economy', the very purpose of economics is to predict the economic consequences of political decisions. That we shall have little to say about the influence of politics upon the economy should not be interpreted as a denial of its existence or importance. Rather, the book is directed to a different, less studied, but in my opinion not less important, question.

The economic model is cut off from the rest of society in that it abstracts from and ignores the effects of the economy upon our personality, behaviour, art, literature, ethics and, above all, our political arrangements. with the result that the attention of economists has been systematically turned away from these phenomena. The purpose of any model is to give the investigator a sense of what is important and what is not. Thus, the success of the model of economic science in directing attention towards the critical variables in many economic problems is the other side of the coin of its failure, from our point of view, to focus on the problem of democracy. To be sure, economists have recognized the political consequences of economic policy informally and have asserted from time to time that this or that policy is dangerous because of what it might do to our form of government. What I am asserting is that our formal model has directed us away from this issue and has forestalled its systematic investigation.

The purpose of this book is to bring an element of formal analysis to the problem, and to develop a way of thinking about the economic prerequisite to democracy that will prove useful in the assessment of economic policy. The study consists of a big question and many little ones. The big question is whether socialism or capitalism is the more compatible with democracy. I suspect that one's answer to this question – rather than one's views about the comparative efficiency of socialism and capitalism — determine whether one's politics are on the left or on the right, whether one votes Labour or Conservative in Britain or, though the association is less pronounced, Democrat or Republican in America. But it is only in extreme and unusual circumstances — where, for instance, one must choose whether to support a full-scale revolution or take sides in a civil war — that one is ever called upon to decide between socialism or capitalism as a whole. Normally, it is the little questions — little only by comparison — of tax policy, co-determination in industry, public support of investment, social security, socialized medicine, unemployment insurance, anti-trust and so on — that one is called upon to answer. Our theory about the economic prerequisite to democracy is unlikely to be of much use unless it can give guidance here.

One might try to subsume the little questions in the big one, reasoning that since socialism and capitalism are extremes on a continuum, and since democracy is compatible with, let us say, socialism but not with capitalism, one may predict the effects on democratic government of each and every sort of economic policy according to whether the policy brings society closer to or farther away from the socialist ideal. Though I am broadly sympathetic to this approach, at least, in so far as I feel that day-to-day policy must be conducted in the light of some ideal, however vague, of economic organization, I would be inclined to recognise two difficulties with it. The first is that one cannot say *a priori* that the ideal lies at either extreme. One cannot rule out the possibility that a balanced economy is like a balanced diet, that one needs moderate amounts of socialism and capitalism just as one needs moderate amounts of carbohydrates and fats. A little arsenic, I'm told, is good for you, though a large amount is not. I do not mean to push this analogy very far. All I wish to convey by it is that the proposition that the closer you are to pure socialism, or pure capitalism as the case may be, the easier it becomes to maintain a democratic government must not be taken as axiomatic and needs to be proved in detail.

I would put considerably more weight upon a second consideration. Capitalism and socialism are generic terms covering a wide range of policies and forms of economic organization, some of which may be conducive to democratic government and some not. For instance, the word 'socialism' encompasses among other things the welfare state and the public ownership of the means of production. The two are not entirely unrelated, but one can imagine a society going a long way towards the welfare state, with socialized education and medicine, extensive unemployment insurance, a universal old age pension and considerable equalization of incomes through the tax system, while at the same time maintaining the means of production and the control of industry entirely in the private sector. The opposite case, of public ownership of the means of production without significant elements of the welfare state, is also possible. An analysis of the political consequences of economic policy that takes capitalism and socialism as indivisible wholes may obscure the relation between economics and politics by directing attention away from our real options.

Ideally, this problem should be approched by setting up a formal model of a political and economic system combined — a model with a given technology of production, where people work, deploy their resources, vote, join pressure groups, form political parties, support the *status quo* or engage in revolution in accordance with their interests, where economic policy is reflected in the parameters of the system and where democratic government works well or badly, breaks down or continues indefinitely, depending on the parameters chosen. The reader will find no such model in this book because what I have to say can best be said in a simpler and less formal way. I do, however, make extensive use of a simple model, introduced in the next chapter, of how people might be expected to vote in circumstances where their incomes are at stake. The inferences drawn from the model are then modified, developed and applied to the assessment of economic policy in the rest of the book.

I think it best to begin by specifying some of my assumptions and value judgements. The book is written from the standpoint of *economic determinism*. I am at one with Laski and Hayek and against Schumpeter in believing that the economy cannot be held separate from the rest of society. Economic determinism is an elastic concept. Under the heading, one might consider the influence of economic organization on art and literature, or the fascinating question, more a subject for novels than for economics, though it has been addressed in essays by Frank Knight and in the works of political theorists, of the effect of economic organization on personality and morals.[6] It is at least possible that the experience of living in a society with a given form of economic organization will so shape the personalities of citizens — making them excessively greedy or excessively timid — that they become unsuited to take their places as free men in a democratic society. That is not the subject matter of this book. Our interpretation of economic determinism is more restricted in scope. As is the custom in economic analysis, we take the psychology of the consumer and citizen as given. Our exclusive concern is with the political consequences of economic policy and economic organization.

A distinction needs to be drawn between what might be called 'technical' and 'economic' determinism. Technical determinism is the doctrine that the driving force of society is the technology of the day. A technical determinist might say: show me the blueprints of all the industrial processes in a society, and I will tell you everything else about it. Economic determinism is a more modest doctrine. It starts not with the technology of a society but with its economic organization (the distribution of the ownership of the means of production, the rules of inheritance, the role of the state and so on), and it predicts the form of government and possibly other aspects of society, depending on how widely or narrowly the doctrine is interpreted. The economic determinist says: show me how the economy is organized, and I will tell you everything else about society. I think it fair to say that Marx's materialist conception of history was closer to technical than to economic determinism; the essence of feudalism, for instance, was not just that society chose to have powerful lords and weak serfs, but that the military and agricultural technology of the time required society to be organized as it was. The quotations from Laski and Hayek reflect economic rather than technical determinism, for both authors see society as being able to choose the form of economic organization and as having the viability of democracy determined, or at least very considerably affected, by the choice. This is true of Laski despite the fact that he considered himself a Marxist; my reading of Laski is that he was not particularly interested in engineering and did not consider the choice between capitalism and socialism to be technologically foreclosed.

A distinction need also be drawn between necessary and sufficient conditions for democracy. The reference in the title of the book to 'the economic prerequisite' is intended to convey the impression that democracy will not work except in conjunction with certain constraints upon or characteristics of the economy. The converse of the proposition need not be true at all. The economic prerequisite is no guarantee of democracy, for there may be non-economic prerequisites as well. One cannot rule out the possibility of democracy being overthrown by an external power or a determined minority, regardless of the organization of the economy. Thus, when speaking of economic determinism, I mean no more than that certain types of economic organization may be inconsistent with democracy. I do not assert that there is a unique one-to-one relation between economic and political life. All I really mean by economic determinism is to deny Schumpeter's proposition that you can do as you like with the economy and you can do as you like with the government without the one affecting the other.

A second major premise is what might be called *individualistic communism*. It is customary to draw a distinction between individualism and collectivism as the starting point for an analysis of the organization of society.[7] Either one begins by postulating a collection of individuals, each with his own tastes, resources and interests, and whose interaction determines what the outcome in society will be; or one postulates that society has interests, personality or a will of its own independently of the individuals within it. Adam Smith and the science of economics generally exemplify one stance, while Hegel and Rousseau exemplify the other. This book is solidly individualistic in the sense that only people can have interests, desires, wills or tastes; the one reference to a general will in Chapter 3 is to a situation where all or almost all citizens have perceived interests in common. But I depart from some versions of individualism by rejecting what might be called the *pedlar theory of the social contract*, according to which government is an agreement among men whose property rights are established prior to the contract and whose continued tenure of these rights is necessarily part of the contract itself. I do not postulate that men enter society like pedlars, each pushing in front of him a cart with goods to use or to trade. Rather – and this is the communistic side of individualistic communism – I assume that the national income and the means of production, including one's own labour, are in the first instance at the disposal of the community as a whole. Initially, nobody has the exclusive right to anything. There are no property rights at the outset of our analysis, and if property rights emerge before we are done it is because, and only because, a majority of voters can be found to support the institution of property and to respect the apportionment of total income among citizens that emerges from the existing distribution of property. Thus what goes by the name of the redistribution is not robbing Peter to pay Paul; it is simply one of many equally legitimate ways of dividing the national income among citizens. If one man is rich and another poor, it is as the outcome of rules that society has established and might in its wisdom disestablish tomorrow. We shall have no use whatsoever for Locke's argument that the present distribution of property can be justified as the outcome of a process in which people acquire land and other goods by the application of their own labour power to the material means of production. Even the major premise of that argument – that one has a right to the fruits of one's own labour – is rejected.

The reason for adopting this extreme stance is partly strategic. I am going to argue that an assignment of property rights – admittedly defined more restrictively and with more room for public intervention than the libertarians or pure free enterprisers would allow – is a prerequisite to democracy. Without meaning to deny the classic economic argument that the assignment of property rights is an efficient way to run the economy, I intend to show that property rights are maintained because democracy needs them for its survival, and I do not want the waters muddied with talk of natural rights. The existing assignment of property has no inherent justification. Property may well originate in theft. We accept the historically given assignment of property, in so far as we do accept it, because a radical reassignment would so lower the national income as to make the majority of voters worse off and because, for reasons set out in the course of this book, the nullification of property rights would destroy democratic government. I am not about to argue that wealth cannot be touched at all. I am not making a case against a wealth tax, a progressive income tax or the old age pension. I shall argue, however, that a society that may at a stroke transform a rich man to a poor man, a society with no respect for property, will not be a democratic society. The premise of such an argument has to be that property is fundamentally at the disposal of the community to be used as the legislature decides.

We desist from expropriating the wealthy, not because they have a right to what they own (except in so far as the rules of society confer that right upon them), but because a society prepared to nullify the right it has conferred on the wealthy would be an unattractive one, even for those who are now poor. We do not expropriate the wealthy because it is not in the interest of the majority of voters to do so.

Property, if it is to be justified at all, must be justified in the interest of the propertyless, or at least in the interest of the majority of voters whose property is small by comparison with the great fortunes. Failing that, the rules of property will, and in my opinion should, be modified until the condition holds. And if no adjustment to the rules of property is sufficient, then the institution of property will and should be abolished altogether.

Democracy has been defined in so many ways and for so many purposes that I hesitate to use the word at all. The usage here is somewhat idiosyncratic though not completely out of line with classical definition of the term. I identify democracy with decision-making by majority rule. For the purposes of this book, a society is democratic if the important issues — the choice of leaders and big decisions in social and economic policy — are decided by voting in accordance with rules that enable the larger number of voters on any issue to have their way. The reason for concentrating on majority rule rather than on, for instance, the maintenance of civil rights or the extent of participation in the political process is not so much that the institution of majority rule is valued for its own sake as that it occupies a central position in the chain of causation from the form of economic organization to those virtues, like freedom of speech and the liberty to experiment and innovate, upon which continued economic growth and social development depend and which are commonly associated with democratic government. The chain is from economic organization to government by majority rule to other virtues which are perhaps more important in themselves. The emphasis will be on the first link, though the second will not be ignored altogether.

In speaking of majority rule, I do not feel it necessary to distinguish among systems of voting, such as proportional representation and single-constituency voting, or among the forms of government in Canada, the United States, France, Sweden and other countries one thinks of as democratic. Instead, I follow a procedure, which is common enough in the social sciences, of designing a story or model of the political process with emphasis on certain allegedly common and important features of all varieties of government by majority rule. Whether the model captures enough of the flesh and blood of the political process to make the story interesting and relevant to day-to-day decision-making is a question the reader must answer for himself as we proceed.

I am not particularly concerned about the extent of the franchise. Majority rule refers in this book to the majority of the designated voters, not to the majority of the population. The reason for this choice is that the connection between economic arrangements and the suitability of majority rule as a means of collective decision-making is the same regardless of the extent of the franchise. It makes virtually no difference to our problems whether 18 to 21-year-olds have the vote, whether women may vote or even whether property qualifications are imposed. This is not to deny that the extent of the franchise is important to the disenfranchised groups, or that discontent among the disenfranchised could make democratic government unworkable. It is rather that the problem that is the subject matter of this book is the same regardless of the extent of the franchise, as long as the franchise is not restricted to the point where majority rule shades off into government by a committee. Nor is it necessary for government by majority rule that all matters be decided by that mechanism. In fact, it is a characteristic of governments one commonly thinks of as democratic that the range of issues determined by majority rule is circumscribed by a written or implicit constitution. One way or another, there is identified a *status quo* that can be altered only by a long and complicated legislative procedure or by a vote of considerably more than half the population. It is only where one cannot identify a *status quo* — as, for instance, in the election of leaders or in legislating for situations that are in some sense unique — that majority rule need be strictly applied.

Thus, for the purposes of this book, majority rule encompasses a wide range of electoral procedures, is consistent with considerable limitation of the franchise, and may be restricted in its application when a *status quo* can be identified. The definition of majority rule is so broad, in fact, that the only alternative is government by blind custom, a committee, a monarch or a dictator.

While not denying that some monarchies have been enlightened and some dictatorships have maintained attributes of a free society for limited periods of time, it is my judgement, which I will not attempt to defend here but from which I expect few readers to dissent, that on balance the absence of democracy is in the long run dreadful. The harm done by a Caligula, a Ghengis Kahn, a Hitler, a Stalin or on a smaller scale an Nkrumah, a Castro or an Idi Amin is so great that the risk of the leader turning out like one of these is too large to compensate for the chance that he will prove more moderate. The stultifying effect of even a moderate and humane monarchy or dictatorship is worse than the conflict, faction and indecision one often finds in democratic government. That is the political premise of this book, and the justification for studying the connection between economic organization and the viability of democratic government as though the maintenance of democratic government were itself the ultimate objective of economic and social policy.

In broad outline the argument of the book is as follows. We begin in Chapter 2 with a simple voting model designed to illustrate the proposition that government by majority rule, though necessary for the preservation of what we think of as a good society, is unstable and unworkable unless the range of issues to be settled by majority rule is severely circumscribed. In particular, government by majority rule cannot be relied upon to assign citizens' shares of the national income. Political assignment creates tension and conflict in society and, carried far enough, must lead to the breakdown of democracy and its replacement by another form of government. We introduce the concept of a system of equity as the minimal requirement of an economy compatible with democratic government. Equity is defined formally and its characteristics are discussed.

In Chapter 3 it is shown how the analysis carries over from the simple model to more complex and realistic societies. Among the topics discussed are the types of issues that can be resolved by voting, the distinction between reassignment and redistribution of income, the civil service, social class, the relation among technology, the competitive economy and democratic government, and the disintegration of democracy when the economic prerequisite has been allowed to dissolve.

Once we have introduced the concept of equity, we shall be able to approach the subject of the Laski, Hayek and Schumpeter quotations with a new vocabulary that will, it is hoped, assist us in analysing the different points of view. The question becomes whether capitalism or socialism contains a system of equity. In Chapter 4 it is argued that pure socialism, defined uncompromisingly as the complete ownership of the means of production by the state, contains no system of equity and is therefore inconsistent with democracy. In Chapter 5 it is argued that capitalism does contain a system of equity which, though far from complete or perfect, is probably sufficient to permit democracy to continue. The capitalist system of equity may be strengthened by a degree of redistribution of income, but it is attenuated to some extent by the growth of monopoly, the growth of government, and an increasing ambiguity as to the scope of property rights.

Finally, Chapter 6 is an examination of economic policy in the light of three interacting criteria: efficiency and equality, which are the traditional criteria of economic analysis, and equity as defined in this book. The topics discussed include price and wage control, the comprehensive tax base, public ownership of firms, socialized medicine, self-management and the subsidization of investment. In some cases, it is shown how considerations of equity can explain policies and institutions. In other cases it is argued that policies adopted to promote efficiency, equality or the interests of subgroups of the population may have the unintended consequence of attenuating the system of equity so that democratic government becomes more difficult and costly to maintain.

2

How a System of Equity enables Society to Cope with the Instability of Democracy: a Simple Case

A pure democracy, by which I mean a society consisting of a small number of citizens, who assemble and administer the government in person, can admit of no cure for the mischiefs of faction. A common passion or interest will, in almost every case, be felt by a majority of the whole; a communication and concert result from the form of government itself; and there is nothing to check the inducements to sacrifice the weaker party or an obnoxious individual. Hence, it is that such democracies have ever been spectacles of turbulence and contention; have ever been found incompatible with personal security or the rights of property; and have in general been as short in their lives as they have been violent in their deaths.

James Madison[1]

Government by majority rule is necessary but deeply flawed: necessary as to a means to preserve the kind of society we wish to live in, for the alternative is dictatorship; flawed, as will be shown in this chapter, because it cannot be used to assign income to citizens. Assignment of income by majority rule would erode the consensus in the community according to which the minority abides by the decision of the majority in every vote. The connection between the form of economic organization and the viability of democratic government lies in the capacity of the economy to compensate for the basic weakness in democratic government.

Democratic government can proceed despite its inability to apportion income among citizens if, and only if, the economy can be depended upon to do the job, that is, if the economy contains within it a mechanism for determining how the national income is assigned. In saying this, I do not mean to imply that government cannot influence the distribution at all. Quite the contrary, I see a substantial role for the government in the redistribution of income, narrowing the gap between rich and poor. But the wholesale determination, through voting, of who shall be rich and who shall be poor is impossible, and government by majority rule gets progressively more difficult the greater the share of each man's income dependent on the outcome of the vote. This proposition and its implications will be illustrated in this chapter in what may at first seem an overly simple and artificial example. It will be shown in the next chapter that the inference we draw from the example carries over, with modification, to more complex and realistic situations. The exploration of the full consequence of the example constitutes the subject matter of the book.[2]

Imagine a community of 15 people organized into a democracy where all decisions are reached through voting and where strict and unlimited majority rule prevails. To show what happens when a democratic government attempts to apportion income among citizens, we abstract from production and suppose instead that the national income of $300,000 falls upon the community like manna from heaven, and that the community has no choice but to vote on the apportionment of the $300,000 among citizens. We also suppose, as economists are accustomed to do, that all men are greedy and that each man is prepared to use the voting mechanism to maximize his share of the common pie. An approximation to such a community might be a democratically governed state where oil royalties are the only source of income.

How might income be assigned in this society? The interesting feature of the example is that, though such a society is conceivable – the income might accrue in a lump to the community, and people may choose to govern themselves democratically – the assignment cannot be predicted from the information supplied.

One's first thought is to suppose that the income might be assigned 'fairly', each man receiving a fifteenth part of the total, amounting to $20,000 per year. But that outcome is unstable in the sense that a majority of voters can be found to support a different assignment more favourable to themselves. Remember that all men are assumed to be greedy without limit. An assignment where each man is awarded $20,000 is unstable because it can be blocked by another assignment, in which at least eight voters, a majority, are better off. A coalition consisting of, say, Mr 1 to Mr 8 agrees to support a bill to the effect that total income is divided equally among the members of the coalition with nothing left over for voters outside the coalition; Mr 1 to Mr 8 each get $37,500 and Mr 9 to Mr 15 each get nothing. Clearly, this outcome is preferable to members of the majority coalition, and the method by which it is achieved is entirely within the rules of collective decision-making.

There is nothing in the example to tell us who the members of the majority coalition will be; our choice of Mr 1 to Mr 8 was completely arbitrary, and any set of eight people would have done as well. The fortunate eight may turn out to be the first eight people to sign a pact, as the survivors of a group of unacquainted rats thrown together in an enclosed space turn out to be the first pair of male and female rats to come together and fight as a team.[3] What is more likely is that some identifiable characteristic will take on political significance. The badge identifying members of the coalition could be French against English or English against French, Hindu against Muslim or Muslim against Hindu, or, best of all, Black against White or White against Black. The point is that the possibility of forming a coalition, and the fear that others may do so, provides an incentive to emphasize and develop differences among people that might otherwise be politically irrelevant.

It was not necessary to suppose men to be very greedy to make the example work. Fear would have done just as well. Consider once again the 'fair' solution where each man gets $20,000. I may be content with that solution and quite willing not to join a coalition designed to raise my income as long as I am confident that all other citizens will behave the same way. But I may join a coalition none the less if I fear that others are about to organize behind my back, for the consequence of exclusion is to lose my income altogether. And like a self-fulfilling prophecy, my approaches to other citizens to form a coalition, or my inquiries as to whether one is about to be formed, provokes the coalition I fear as my intentions become suspect.

The coalition of Mr 1 to Mr 8, once formed, may or may not be stable depending on the degree of foresight of the members of the coalition. Consider the position of Mr 9 to Mr 15. As an alternative to having no income at all, they may try to break the coalition of Mr 1 to Mr 8 by detaching one member, say Mr 8, and offering him something in excess of $37,500. They may, for instance, offer him $90,000 to form a new majority coalition voting for an assignment in which Mr 1 to Mr 7 get nothing, Mr 8 gets $90,000, and each of Mr 9 to Mr 15 gets $30,000. Whether Mr 8 accepts the offer depends on what he predicts will happen next. He would certainly accept if guaranteed that the second coalition will hold because the increase in his income is substantial. But there is no reason to believe that it will, for it can be blocked by a third coalition composed of Mr 1 to Mr 7 together with one person from the group consisting of Mr 9 to Mr 15 (it does not matter who); or Mr 9 to Mr 15 may attempt to replace Mr 8 with one person from the group consisting of Mr 1 to Mr 7, all of whom will accept an income well below $90,000 as an alternative to exclusion from the coalition. In fact, it can be shown that no stable coalition can ever emerge as long as a citizen is prepared to enter a new coalition whenever he can increase his income by so doing. Any coalition is dominated by some other coalition in which each member of the latter can make himself better off than he was before.

On this assumption, the voting goes on indefinitely and democratic government breaks down because there is, literally, no assignment that will not be overturned in the very next vote.[4]

If Mr 8 understands this process, as he undoubtedly would, he will not be tempted to leave the first coalition no matter how much he is offered to join Mr 9 to Mr 15 because he knows that he will not get to keep what he is offered on the second round. The ultimate consequence of his defection will be either the establishment of a new coalition in which he may or may not participate or the failure of the voting mechanism to assign incomes at all. Mr 8 rejects the offer of Mr 9 to Mr 15, and the voting mechanism yields the only possible outcome that is stable on the assumptions we have made — an assignment where a bare majority coalition shares the whole national income among its members and citizens outside the coalition get nothing. Income is divided equally among the members of the coalition because each man knows that the other members of the coalition would have an incentive to replace him if his income were higher than the rest. Thus we arrive at a result that is perhaps surprising and certainly unappealing. If the assignment of the national income is to be decided by majority rule and all citizens are prepared to abide by the outcome of the vote regardless of the consequences to themselves, then the only stable outcome is one where just under half the population is deprived of income altogether.

This is not the end of the story. If assignment of incomes by majority rule is as unattractive to the minority as this example would lead one to believe, then our major premise, that everyone accepts the outcome of the vote, cannot be right. The minority would eventually refuse to accept the assignment as binding upon itself and would use every available means to induce the majority to treat it more favourably. Though there is as yet no mechanism within the terms of our example by which pressure might be exerted, it is not difficult to imagine how the example might be extended to make this possible. One might introduce some of the characteristics of bargaining in industrial relations by supposing that each citizen, on pressing a certain button, can reduce the national income to some extent. Or one might allow citizens to fight among themselves on the assumption that the fight, if it occurs, is unpleasant for everyone and that better organization or greater strength and determination may enable the minority to win. Under these circumstances, it would be in the interest of the majority to muster its strength to suppress the minority or to reduce the danger of rebellion by conceding more income to the minority than would be in the interest of the majority to concede if the outcome of the vote were accepted without protest.

It is now very difficult to say what the assignment of incomes would be, for the assignment has come to depend on the strength and determination of the contending groups. This much is clear. What began as assignment by voting has degenerated into assignment by threat and force, a process in which democracy is little more than a facade and may well be abolished altogether by a group in power unwilling to risk losing that power at the ballot box.

Our analysis of voting has got us into deeper and deeper water. We first supposed that income was assigned equally. This gave way, through self-interested voting, to an assignment from which the minority was excluded. This in turn gave way either to a situation where the legislature finds itself unable to agree on any assignment of incomes, or to one where the assignment reflects an ill-defined balance of force almost regardless of the voting mechanism. Whatever we assume, it turns out that the attempt to assign incomes by voting gives rise to consequences so unacceptable that the voting mechanism itself would sooner or later be abandoned. The voting mechanism, indispensable though it may be to keep the dictator at bay, destroys itself when used to apportion income among citizens. It is convenient to refer to this phenomenon as *the problem of faction*, a usage that was common in the eighteenth century when democracy was still suspect and mixed government, with elements of monarchy and democracy, was often preferred.

The political implication seems inescapable. If the legislature cannot assign incomes peacefully, it must not be allowed to do so at all. To keep the voting mechanism for the election of leaders and for specifying the content of the law, we must restrict its application so that the difficulties we have been discussing do not arise. We must ensure that assignment is attended to outside of and, at least in part, independently of the political process. In fact, every democratic society imposes restrictions on the voting mechanism in a constitution or in a set of customs and traditions that for all practical purposes has the force of a constitution and that cannot be abandoned if democratic government is to continue.[5] Perhaps most important among such restrictions are the guarantees of civil rights – freedom of speech, freedom from arbitrary arrest and so on – that are intended to protect minorities from majorities and that, if effective, go a long way towards preserving democratic government by removing the grounds for the fear that each man might otherwise feel about the intentions of his neighbours. But we are not concerned with civil liberties in this book. Our concern is with a related and complementary mechanism in the economy.

Let us suppose, contrary to what we have so far assumed, that there is in our 15-man society a traditional and established method of assigning the available income to citizens. Technically, if majority rule prevails, the majority in the legislature could refuse to recognize the method and could appropriate the whole income for itself in the manner discussed above. But the majority — all potential majorities — may desist and show restraint, choosing instead to honour the established method of assigning incomes to people because everyone understands full-well what the political consequences of any other course of action would be and because more importance is attached to the preservation of democratic government than to temporary gain from collusive behaviour.

It is appropriate at this point to introduce the term *equity*, which will be used extensively throughout the book and which, as the reader was warned in the preface, is defined in a specific, technical sense, different in certain respects from the common meaning of the term today. A *system of equity* is a means society employs to assign incomes to people, outside of and prior to the political process. A system of equity is what our 15-man society requires to remove the assignment of income from the political arena and so preserve democracy for those kinds of decisions — the choice of leaders, the formation of laws and even, as we shall see, the reduction of the spread between the incomes of rich and poor — for which democratic procedures are possible. Along with the term 'equity', we can define *inequity* as the violation by government or legislature of the established rules for assigning incomes to people, and the *absence of equity* as a situation where the legislature, monarch or central committee must assign incomes to people because there is no alternative means, no system of equity, to do the job.

The 15-man community might have adopted any of several systems of equity, most of which may seem a little bizarre because the economy in our example is bizarre, but which have their obvious generalizations in more realistic circumstances. The community might have agreed upon a *feudal* system of equity in which citizens are assigned to social classes with unequal shares of the national income. For instance, there may be five members of the upper class who get $30,000 each, five members of the middle class who get $20,000 each, and five members of the lower class who get $10,000 each. One might associate the classes with roles in state ceremonials, or with positions in government that 'require' different incomes, as a judge is considered to require a reasonably high income to insure against his becoming dishonest. The distinguishing features of feudal equity are that everyone would prefer to be upper class than to be middle class and to be middle class than to be lower class, and that positions in these classes are inherited.

The community might have agreed upon a *capitalistic* system of equity. Instead of collecting the manna as it falls from heaven and dividing the whole pile among citizens in some allegedly appropriate way, the community might divide up the land where the manna is expected to fall and allow each man to keep the manna that falls on his territory. Only an historian knows how the division of land has come to be what it is.

Theft, exploitation, inheritance, sale and gift may have all played a role in creating the existing distribution. But the community accepts the distribution as it is because each man knows what a Pandora's box would be opened if the system of equity were challenged successfully.

The community might have agreed on *equality* as a system of equity. The common income of $300,000 is used to provide $20,000 for each of the 15 citizens. This, as I see it, is obviously the best system and the one most likely to be accepted in the simple economy we have been considering, but, as will be shown later on, it would prove unworkable in more complex economies where production and distribution have both to be considered.

And, to end our list, the community might agree on a *patriarchial* system of equity, where a planner is empowered to assign income among citizens in accordance with his perception of the norm, customs and morals of the community. Each citizen might be entitled to an extra large income in those years when his needs are correspondingly large, as when he requires medical attention or has to send his children to college. The difficulties with such a system are obvious. The patriarch must possess considerable power over the rest of the population, and it is hard to imagine how the voting problems we have been discussing can be avoided in his appointment, how he can be prevented from using that power in his own interest, and how a line is to be drawn between the powers of the patriarch and matters to be decided by the will of the majority in a free vote.

Each of these methods of apportioning the national income might be thought of as a candidate for a system of equity, but it is not yet clear which if any would actually do the job of preserving democratic government by arranging the assignment of incomes outside of and independently of the legislature. A way to test these and other candidates for a system of equity is to specify the characteristics of equity and then to see whether the characteristics are present in the proposed methods of assignment. A system of equity would seem to require two characteristics: it must be *feasible*, and it must be *acceptable*.

A proposed assignment is feasible as a system of equity if it has no loose ends, if it does not require political intervention at some stage to determine who gets what. A proposed assignment is feasible as a system of equity if the national income and all of the advantages in society are divided up among citizens with nothing left over for the legislature to dispose. Feasibility is not an all-or-nothing criterion, for if it were we should have to say that the only feasible system of equity is one so comprehensive that democratic government would be eliminated altogether. The choice of leaders has a pronounced effect upon the welfare of candidates for office, and any act of legislature affects the assignment of income to some extent. Decisions about how to build public buildings affect the incomes of carpenters, artists and stone masons. Reduction of military expenditure is harmful to workers and owners of firms in defence industries and beneficial to workers and owners of firms in other sectors of the economy. A distinction can none the less be made between a society where the great majority of people are confident that their income and status will be in large measure independent of the political process, and a society where each man feels that his income and status may be significantly affected by tomorrow's vote. Faction cannot be eliminated altogether, but democratic government can be preserved as long as there is a non-political mechanism in society determining a large enough share of the incomes of a large enough proportion of the population that the residual income, which must be assigned within the legislature, is not worth fighting about.

We can think of the *degree of feasibility* of a system of equity as the proportion of a man's total expected income he can count on regardless of what the legislature decides. Thus, if a man knows that his wage next year will be not less than $80 per day and not more than $120, with an equal chance of any income between these limits (depending, for instance, on how high a tariff the legislature chooses to establish on imports in competition with the produce of his labour), we can say that the degree of feasibility, for him, is 80 percent, $80 being the minimum he is assured prior to and independently of what the legislature may decide, and $100 being his expected income once the behaviour of the legislature is taken into account. It should be borne in mind, however, that the degree of feasibility is not a concept like distance or time that can be measured exactly. The effect of political decision-making on income varies from person to person and from vote to vote; some votes may affect one's income a great deal and others hardly at all. The degree of feasibility is just a heuristic device to explain that a system of equity may govern the assignment of income to a greater or lesser extent.[6]

The concept of the degree of feasibility is helpful, despite the spurious precision, as a way of emphasizing that the problem in the design of economic policy is not to create a perfect and complete system of equity — for the system is never perfect or complete — but to maintain a degree of feasibility sufficient for the preservation of democratic government. The working hypothesis of this book is that reasonable men can split the difference, even in a voting context, as long as the amount at stake for any individual is small by comparison with the part of his income he can count on regardless of the outcome of the vote; the mischief of faction increases as the degree of feasibility declines; and democracy breaks down, as in our 15-man example, if the degree of feasibility is allowed to fall below some limit. We cannot say where precisely is the limit on the scale from perfect equity to full political assignment of income. What we can do is analyse economic policy in accordance with its effect of the degree of feasibility and acceptability of the system of equity as a whole and, on occasion, to argue that such-and-such a set of economic arrangements is clearly above or clearly below any conceivable line.

Of the proposed systems of equity outlined above — feudal, capitalist, equality and patriarchal — the first three are perfectly feasible in the artificial economy in our example, for they leave the legislature with no influence on the assignment of incomes at all. The fourth is feasible if and only if a patriarch can be found. If not, if an ordinary, greedy citizen must be chosen to play the role of patriarch, and if the actions of each candidate for the office of patriarch can be predicted, then all of the difficulties of assignment by voting arise in the choice of a patriarch, and the proposed system of equity is infeasible.

The other essential characteristic of a system of equity is acceptability. A method of assigning income cannot serve as a system of equity unless it is accepted by the legislature. There is of course no guarantee that the legislature will respect a given rule for assignment of income, and it would therefore be pointless to define a system of equity in such a way that a guarantee is required. What I mean by acceptability is somewhat different. I mean that a situation will not arise where over 50 per cent of the legislature stands to gain in the long run by using its voting power to overturn the method of assignment in force. A method of assignment is acceptable in this sense if the cost to the poorest 50 per cent of the population of the general disorganization of society that would result if assignment were overturned exceeds what they might gain from the displacement of the old upper class. A method of assignment will not serve as a system of equity unless voters are confident that it will be preserved, at least for the most part and for a substantial period of time, because if the system is going to break down tomorrow, it is in the interest of each voter to establish a coalition today as a way of maximising his chances of coming out on top in whatever new arrangements eventually emerge. There are candidates for a system of equity which are feasible in the sense that income would be assigned outside of the political arena if all voters accepted the rules, but which would fail in practice because the rules would not be accepted by a majority of voters. Acceptability is a difficult characteristic to pin down as it depends at least in part upon the moral and social characteristics of voters, but an example will show what is involved.

Imagine, in our 15-man, $300,000 society, that there has been established a feudal tradition in which one man gets $160,000 per year and all others get $10,000 per year. The tradition is entirely feasible as a system of equity in the sense that the legislature need not concern itself with the assignment of incomes. It is not likely to be acceptable for long. Sooner or later, greed, envy or a sense of injustice will lead the 14 men with incomes of $10,000 to protest against the traditions of their society, insisting that the prize position be rotated among citizens (for all practical purposes, the conversion of feudal equity into equality, because men would then be equal over their lifetimes), or that feudal equity be done away with altogether and replaced with some more generally acceptable arrangement. Real feudalism emerged in circumstances where social classes corresponded to economic and military tasks and where possession of weapons gave the military classes a decisive advantage over the rest of society. Though there were rudimentary parliaments, there was nothing like majority rule and no one dreamed of governing society by a legislature in which lord and serf each had one vote. The statement by Laski quoted at the beginning of Chapter 1 can be interpreted to mean that capitalistic equity is no more acceptable than feudal equity because the inequality of the capitalist system would prove intolerable in a democratic society.

Our enumeration of possible systems of equity may convey the impression that society has a number of alternatives to choose from and that the problem is to find the system most suited to current needs. That is not so. Rather, as will become evident when we pass in the following chapters from the simple example to a more realistic portrait of society, there appears to be no practical alternative to the system of equity currently in force; the existing system is complex, and the degree of feasibility is already dangerously low, though it may be raised somewhat by the judicious choice of economic policy.[7]

The meaning of the word 'equity' in this book will be misunderstood — and the whole line of argument we are making correspondingly distorted — unless it is borne in mind that the word is being used in a special and technical sense, distinct from though not entirely unrelated to the common everyday meaning of the term. The earliest usage of the term was as a principle for modifying the letter of the law when the spirit and intent would seem to be violated in a strict reading of the code.[8] Courts of equity were established in late medieval England to rectify the deficiencies of the common law. In practice, courts of equity tended to specialize in the law of property, and the principles of equity pertained to questions of inheritance or the resolution of commercial disputes. A distinction between law and equity is still recognized, though the separate courts of equity were abolished a century ago. A residue of this development is to be found in the use of the word 'equity' to describe the size of one's share of the value of a firm. One also speaks of having such and such an equity in one's house, or, somewhat more distant from its legal origin, of debt and equity as the two main types of financial instruments. Something of the legal overtones of the term remain in our usage in this book.

The word 'equity' is used in public finance to denote characteristics of the tax structure.[9] A tax structure is said to be horizontally equitable if a farmer who earns $30,000 pays neither more nor less tax, because he is a farmer, than a lawyer who also earns $30,000; a tax structure is said to be vertically equitable if its effect is to cause the spread between net, after-tax, incomes to be narrower than the spread between gross incomes. The meaning of equity in the phrase 'horizontal equity' is close to the meaning in this book but much more restricted in the range of circumstances to which it applies.

Recently there has been a tendency to use the word 'equity' as a fancy synonym for equality; in this usage, a change in the distribution of income is said to be equitable if the rich get poorer and the poor get richer. This usage is unfortunate, because the word 'equality' already denotes what equity has come to mean, and because it would be helpful to preserve the legal and conventional overtones of the term.

These usages must be carefully distinguished from the usage in this book. A system of equity for the purposes of this book is not necessarily just by any absolute standard, though it is unlikely to be perceived as grossly unjust by a majority of voters. Nor does a system of equity require that incomes be equal, though a gross departure from equality might corrode the acceptability of the system. Equity is no more than a non-political means of assigning income, a means that may be just and may be conducive to equality but need not, strictly speaking, be either in order to do its job of keeping the problem of faction at bay in a democratic society.

Equity is inevitably a conservative virtue. It specifies a *status quo* that society may accept or modify but cannot reject outright if democratic government is to be preserved, except in those rare instances where everyone, or almost everyone, can agree to substitute one system of equity for another. For there is at bottom no best, most just or most efficient assignment of income among citizens. The abandonment of the traditional means of assignment must lead to the development of faction, the threats and the civil strife that the system of equity is designed to avoid. Yet the system of equity does change, painfully. Prior to 1860 it was consistent with the system of equity in the United States for one man to own another; five years later that was no longer so. The enclosures that occurred gradually in England during the sixteenth, seventeenth and eighteenth centuries can be thought of as a change from a system of equity where the different classes take traditionally prescribed shares in the produce of the land to one where land is fully owned by one party and labour is fully owned by another. The change was brought about with less conflict than might be expected because the franchise was restricted to give disproportionate voting power to the social class that had most to gain from the change. More recently, the introduction of socialized medicine, unemployment insurance, social security, rent control, price and wage control, and many changes in the prerogatives of property can all be looked upon as modifications of the prevailing system of equity.

Change may support equity if it transforms a system that has come to be thought of as unjust or unacceptable to a great many citizens, and is generally believed to be insecure, to a new system that commands more universal support and is expected to hold for the foreseeable future. Land reform may occasionally represent a change to a new, more solid system of equity. Prior to reform, the landless peasants constitute a block of voters with an interest in shifting income from landowner to labour and from rich to poor in every available way; the reform creates a solid core of small peasants with an interest in the preservation of property rights. The expropriation of the Zamindari in India may be an instance of this phenomenon. The Zamindari originated as tax farmers in the Mogul dynasty, gained clear title to their lands under the British, and had a questionable claim to their land once Independence was achieved. Their tenants, transformed into small landowners, immediately acquired a stake in society as it was. On the other hand, land reform may be used to eliminate an obstreperous social class rather than to create the economic requirements of democratic government. Land reform in China was no more than a stage in the establishment of collective farms. Whether a particular change in economic institutions leads to a strengthening or deterioration of the system of equity cannot be determined *a priori*; it depends on the circumstances of the case.

The meaning of the concept of equity may be clarified by considering an objection that may occur to the reader at this point: the distinction between assignment of income in the legislature and assignment in accordance with a system of equity might be considered artificial or irrelevant because the legislature can overturn the system of equity at any time and the decision not to do so is itself a sort of political assignment. It is just as much political assignment to let the system of equity stand as to abolish or replace it. A legislature, choosing to abide by, let us say, a capitalist system of equity and knowing the full implications of its choice, has in effect assigned incomes to citizens exactly as if there had been no system of equity and the incomes and status of citizens were determined by a simple majority vote. If this be so, it is hard to see why calling the resulting configuration of incomes a system of equity should alleviate the difficulties with assignment by majority rule.

Against this argument, I would defend the concept of equity by observing that a system of equity, if there is one, provides the legislature with an option it does not otherwise have. The legislature may quietly and tacitly agree not to discuss the assignment of incomes at all. If there is a system of equity, each member of the legislature may say to himself that, while he is less than fully content with his portion under the existing arrangement, he had better accept the arrangement because the social disruption, the conflict among legislators and the threat to the continuance of democratic government when the legislature chooses to concern itself with the assignment of income to citizens is too high a price to pay for whatever improvement in his position he can expect in the new assignment, especially as he must, unless he is very poor, reckon with a substantial probability of his exclusion from the new winning coalition and of his becoming worse off than he would be if the system of equity were respected. If most voters reason this way, the system of equity will hold and there will be no mention of assignment in the deliberations of the legislature, even in the case where the assignment entailed by the system of equity would be rejected if it had emerged in the process of political assignment described above. Accept the system of equity, and nothing more need be decided. Reject it, and the legislature is plunged into a conflict that cannot be resolved.

There is a sense in which a system of equity is found or inherited but not chosen. In the objection we are considering, equity is looked upon as though the legislature chose a system exactly as it might choose a particular assignment of incomes. Typically, that is not the way equity works at all. Citizens are born into a society with a pre-existing system of equity that they can, but need not, modify or replace. Equity has evolved, like the institution of money or culture, together with the history of society as a whole. Its evolution was accompanied by conflict and disharmony, and it may be thought of as part of the overhead capital of society on which we have come to depend and which we may improve, diminish or destroy altogether according to the policies we choose to adopt.

3

Extension to a Complex Society

By directing that industry in such a manner as its produce may be of the greatest value, he intends only his own gain, and he is in this, as in many other cases, led by an invisible hand to promote an end which was no part of his intention.

Adam Smith[1]

A decentralized economy motivated by self-interest and guided by price signals would be compatible with a coherent disposition of economic resourses. . . . It is important to understand how surprising this claim must be to anyone not exposed to this tradition. The immediate 'common sense' answer to the question 'What will an economy motivated by a very large number of different agents look like?' is probably: There will be chaos . . . . quite a different answer has long been claimed true and has indeed permeated the economic thinking of a large number of people who are in no way economists.

Kenneth Arrow and
Frank Hahn[2]

The role of equity as a link between economic organization and the viability of democratic government has so far been illustrated in a model of society without production, bureaucracy, social class, pressure groups or representative government and where the range of issues about which the community might vote is so restricted that nothing is left over when the assignment of incomes to citizens is removed; the system of equity supplants voting altogether. Yet I shall argue that the main propositions in the last chapter — that the legislature cannot assign incomes, that democratic government requires a system of equity, and that economic policy can be assessed according to its effect in strengthening or attenuating the system of equity — do carry over from the simple society in our example to more complex and realistic societies. To make such a case, it is necessary to study how the analysis might be extended or modified to account for facets of real societies we have so far overlooked. We begin with voting itself in an attempt to specify what a democratic society can be expected to vote on amicably. Then we consider how the conclusions drawn from our simple example need be modified to take account of additional aspects of society and government. And finally, in the light of our more comprehensive picture of society, we discuss briefly how democratic government may break down if no system of equity is recognized or if the degree of feasibility is low.

WHAT WE VOTE ABOUT

It is convenient to identify three types of issues that might be subject to a vote: matters of general concern, single-peaked issues, and a residual class of issues to be called factional because they may give rise to factions as described in Chapter 2. In matters of general concern, there is a right course of action for the community as a whole, a general will if you like, but views differ as to what it is. The election of a president is a matter of general concern in this sense when the policies of the candidates are secondary, and the important questions have to do with the qualities of the candidates themselves. Who is the more competent man? Who is likely to run the most effective counter-cyclical policy? Who will be the shrewdest in negotiation with other countries? Who is likely to make the wisest decisions on matters of peace and war? The election of a president ceases to be a matter of general concern as defined here and acquires some of the character of single-peaked or factional issues when the different candidates become identified with policies appealing to different social classes or pressure groups. Other matters of general concern arise in law reform, where most voters anticipate that they are more likely to be affected as victims than as perpetrators of crime. Decisions about the severity of penalties, judicial discretion in sentencing or the powers of parents over children are usually matters of this kind. The defining characteristic of such issues is not that the majority is necessarily right in its judgement, but that it suffers together and equally with the minority if it is wrong. It should be recognized, of course, that to speak of matters of general concern is to describe an ideal type to which actual cases may be more or less closely approximated. It is hard to imagine any issue in which nobody stands to gain or lose more than his neighbours from the outcome of the vote. At a minimum, elections matter a great deal to the candidates and the consequences of changing the severity of sentences are different for criminals than for the public at large. But the losers in such cases are either unidentified when the issue is resolved or too few in number to influence the outcome of a vote in the legislature.

An issue is single-peaked if all possible outcomes may be associated with numbers on a scale, where each voter (i) has a preferred number, and (ii) having to choose between outcomes corresponding to two other numbers, both above or both below his preferred number, will always vote for the outcome closest to his preferred number.[3] For example, suppose five men are voting on the size of the old age pension. Mr 1 would like it to be $100, Mr 2 would like it to be $200, Mr 3 would like it to be $300, Mr 4 would like it to be $400 and Mr 5 would like it to be $500. Mr 5 who would like to see the old age pension set at $500, would vote for an old age pension of $400 if the only alternative were an old age pension of $300, while Mr 1, given the same alternatives, would vote for a pension of $300. It is evident, in this example, what the old age pension will be: it will be $300, because Mr 3 can find a coalition to vote down any other sum while no coalition can be formed against $300. Mr 3 can form a coalition with Mr 1 and Mr 2 against any number greater than $300, and he can form a coalition with Mr 4 and Mr 5 against any number less. Notice particularly the contrast between this example, where the outcome of the voting is nicely determinate, and the example of 15 men assigning a sum of money in the last chapter, where no comparable outcome could be discovered. In general, single-peaked issues have the properties that there is a unique outcome of the voting process, that the decision of the legislature is in accordance with the preference of the median voter (the voter whose preferred outcome is such that there are as many voters to the left of him as to the right) and that strategy or faction can have no effect upon the outcome of the vote as long as voters are rational.

There are many single-peaked issues. That the determination of the size of the old age pension may be such an issue is demonstrated in our example. The amount of unemployment insurance is another. The progressivity of the income tax is not quite single-peaked, but is probably close enough that the setting of rates of tax is more like the setting of the amount of the old age pension than like the allocation of $300,000 among 15 men. The setting of tax rates is strictly single-peaked if, and in so far as, the progressivity of the tax system can be expressed as one number and voting is restricted to the determination of 'the' rate of progressivity. The determination of the tax structure ceases to be single-peaked for marginal adjustments that affect rates in the different tax brackets without affecting the overall progressivity of the system. A given rate of progressivity may, for instance, be consistent with *either* a relatively high rate on the bracket from $40,000 to $50,000 and a relatively low rate on the bracket from $50,000 to $60,000, *or* a relatively low rate on the first bracket and a relatively high rate on the second. The choice between these options begins to look like the example in the last chapter. The reason why small changes in the tax schedule do not normally provoke the sort of conflict described there is that the amounts of money involved are probably quite small when we adhere to the rule that the marginal tax rate shall rise steadily with income.

Factional issues are those that are neither matters of general concern nor single-peaked. The name 'factional' is chosen to denote this residual category because only when preferences are single-peaked is it advantageous to vote straightforwardly and according to one's preferences, with nothing to gain from factions, coalitions or strategic behaviour. Just as one can treat the choice of the size of the old age pension as the prototype of a single-peaked issue, so, for the purposes of this book, can one think of the 15-man example in Chapter 2 as the prototype of a factional issue. The essential feature of that example was that it was not possible to line up all assignments of incomes to people – as one can line up all magnitudes of the old age pension – so that each man has a preferred position on the line and an incentive, in a vote between two possible outcomes both to the left or both to the right of his preferred outcome, to vote for the outcome closest to his first preference. No median voter can be identified, and there is no preferred outcome of the legislature dependent simply upon the preferences of the voters and independent of the coalitions that arise in the voting process.

Voting on factional issues may not even be determinate. There is a well-known paradox of voting according to which no course of action is chosen over all other courses of action in a sequence of pairwise votes despite the fact each man's preferences among the options are well specified. The standard demonstration of this possibility is in a vote among three options, x, y and z, in a legislature with three members, Mr 1, Mr 2, and Mr 3. Suppose Mr 1 prefers x to y to z, Mr 2 prefers y to z to x, and Mr 3 prefers z to x to y.

In legislation over the form of industrial organization, option x might be to keep the present system where firms are controlled by boards of directors appointed by shareholders, option y might be worker control of firms, option z might be a mixed system in which appointed civil servants have a great deal of influence; a class of rich men might play the role of Mr 1, socialist workers might play the role of Mr 2, and civil servants might play the role of Mr 3. The rich men (1) prefer the present system (x) to worker control (y) to the mixed system (z). The socialist workers (2) prefer worker control (y) to the mixed system (z) to the present system (x). The civil servants (3) prefer the mixed system (z) to the present system (x) to worker control (y). The three classes have approximately equal voting strength.

Voting in accordance with simple majority rule is indeterminate in this case because the voting procedure yields a set of preferences for the community that would be irrational in an individual, despite the fact that no individual is irrational. We can see at once that the community

— as represented in the legislature — prefers x to y, and y to z, but none the less prefers z to x. The option x wins in a vote with y because Mr 1 and Mr 3 both prefer x to y; y wins in a vote with z because Mr 1 and Mr 2 both prefer y to z; but x fails to win in a vote with z because Mr 2 and Mr 3 both prefer z to x. In this situation, everything depends on legislative rules. Nothing can be resolved unless the voting can be terminated at some point, and any outcome can be engineered by an appropriate ordering of votes. The rules committee can manipulate the community to vote for y, for instance, by first eliminating x in a pair-wise vote between x and z and then pitting y against z. Comparable sequences can be worked out to make the community vote for x or z.

In the light of this simple typology of voting, we can now make what will prove to be an important distinction between reassignment and redistribution of income. A change in income is a redistribution if the gap between rich and poor is reduced but the ordering of incomes is preserved. A change is a reassignment if there is a reordering of people on the scale of rich and poor. The distinction is illustrated in a three-person example (see Table 3.1). Originally, as shown in column (0), Mr 1 has an income of $10,000, Mr 2 has an income of $20,000, and Mr 3 has an income of $30,000. The change shown in column (1) is a pure redistribution because the ordering of incomes is unchanged but spread between the highest and lowest incomes is reduced. The change shown in column (2) is a pure reassignment because the ordering has changed while the dispersion has not. The change shown in column (3) is redistribution and reassignment combined.

The reason for contrasting distribution and assignment is that what appears to the statistician as identical changes in the distribution of income may have entirely different political and social consequences. The statistician can observe shares of total income accruing to each decile of the population, and he can say whether the gap between rich and poor is narrowing over time. He can tell whether the economy is changing

Table 3.1. The distinction between reassignment and redistribution of income

		(0) Original assignment $(000)	(1) Redistribution $(000)	(2) Reassignment without redistribution $(000)	(3) Reassignment with redistribution $(000)
Mr	1	10	15	30	25
Mr	2	20	20	20	20
Mr	3	30	25	10	15

in a manner comparable to a change from the original assignment (column (0)) in the table to an assignment like column (1) or (3) where the spread between the high income and the low income is reduced. What he cannot observe, at least not from the usual tabulation of tax or income statistics, is whether the change is exclusively redistribution as we have defined it, or redistribution and reassignment together. He cannot distinguish (0) from (2) or (1) from (3).

The political consequences of redistribution and reassignment differ in two respects. First, the absolute size of the gains and losses is greater under reassignment than under redistribution alone. In the passage from column (0) to (1), Mr 1 gains $5,000 and Mr 3 loses $5,000, but in the passage from (0) to (3), Mr 1 gains $15,000 and Mr 3 loses $15,000, despite the fact that (1) and (3) are statistically identical. The prospect of a passage from (0) to (3) will therefore provoke the enthusiastic support of Mr 1 and the equally enthusiastic resistance of Mr 3; it is the setting for a major political conflict. The passage from (0) to (1), on the other hand, will provoke less passion on both sides and may be accepted, or rejected for that matter, with little fuss. The contrast is reinforced by the likelihood that status in the community and the opportunity to do interesting and important work are attached to one's ordering on the scale of rich and poor and are fairly well independent of absolute income. Thus, the passage from (0) to (1) preserves the status of Mr 1, Mr 2 and Mr 3, while the passage from (0) to (3) lowers the status of Mr 3 and raises the status of Mr 1 accordingly.

Second, the choice of the amount of redistribution is within an inch of being a single-peaked issue with a determinate voting equilibrium, while the reassignment of income is a thoroughly factional issue. For each voter, there is a preferred degree of redistribution which is the outcome of a balancing of two considerations: his position on the scale of rich and poor, which would determine whether he wants redistribution at all, and his assessment of the consequences on the efficiency of the economy. One would suppose that redistribution would lower the efficiency of the economy by reducing the incentive to work, save or educate oneself for a better job. Each voter wants income redistributed to the point where what he expects to gain from the increase in his share of income from any extra redistribution is just balanced by what he expects to lose from the resulting decline in total output. The extent of redistribution desired by the median voter is the voting equilibrium for the community as a whole. The argument is entirely analogous to our discussion of the progressivity of the income tax, and the qualifications mentioned there apply here as well.

There is, in other words, a natural limit to redistribution. The man who opposes redistribution can at least take consolation from the fact that each step towards greater redistribution enlists a new cohort of opponents, for whom the adverse effect of the fall in total income outweighs the favourable effect of the redistribution itself, until a majority of voters can be found to oppose its further extension.[5]

Reassignment on the other hand has no comparable limit or stopping place because there is no just price or standard of remuneration over and above what the market supplies. A decision by the legislature to raise the income of a particular trade or region can only serve to weaken the consensus in society as to who has the right to what, increasing the pressure for additional reassignment elsewhere. Thus, for example, a decision to raise the income of farmers − by means of marketing boards, agricultural price supports, or tariffs on the import of food − is immediately confronted with the threefold problem that the legislature has no basis for deciding by how much farm income should be raised, that farmers have no incentive to be satisfied with the legislation on their behalf or to desist from political pressure for additional advantages, and that the special treatment of farmers provokes workers in all other trades and in non-agricultural regions of the country to seek special interest legislation for themselves, through pure emulation and because the rise in the incomes of farmers can only be procured at the expense of other groups in the economy. In sharp contrast to redistribution, the political difficulties with reassignment become more severe with each additional step.

One must, of course, recognize that, as no income can rise to infinity, there have to be forces in society to hold incomes down. The point being made here is that there are forces *within* the voting procedure to control the extent of redistribution, while reassignment can be limited only by appeal to forces *outside* the voting procedure: strikes, propaganda, violence and the capacity of the economy to support the favoured group.

The relevance to equity should be evident. Our classification of issues on which people might vote enables us to sharpen the distinction between matters that can be resolved by voting and matters that must be attended to by a system of equity if democratic government is to be maintained. Voting can be about matters of general concern or about single-peaked issues where the latter includes the determination of the extent of redistribution of income in the economy. Other matters, particularly the basic assignment from which redistribution arises, have to be arranged by other means.

Finally, it should be appreciated that the distinction between single-peaked issues and factional issues is not as sharp as the analysis so far might lead one to believe. Issues can lose their character as single-peaked when combined in the process of logrolling.[6] Taken one by one, the determination of the size of the old age pension, the amount of unemployment insurance, and the amount of transfer to the poor are all single-peaked issues. For instance, each voter has a sense of what he considers to be the appropriate size of the old age pension, and the median voter, who is unlikely to be an old age pensioner himself, can be expected to have his way if the determination of the size of the pension is to be voted upon in isolation from all other issues. But issues are not kept in separate compartments. The old, the unemployed and the poor might easily form a coalition which, alone or in combination with other groups, constitutes a majority of voters and may use its voting power to enhance the incomes of its members at the expense of the rest of society as described in the last chapter.

There is another more hopeful possibility. Issues, some of which are intrinsically single-peaked and some not, may get artificially combined as programmes of political parties. On the face of it, it seems strange that people are inclined to identify political views on a scale of left and right. How, after all, can the vast range of issues confronting our society be aligned with the seating arrangement of the French National Assembly of 1789? Is it at bottom any different from the ancient Chinese classification of all things as *yin* and *yang* or the totism of the North American Indians? Perhaps not, but the left-right distinction may be understood as a subtle device to convert a great collection of what would otherwise be factional issues into one single-peaked issue on which the median voter may, after all, get his way. Somehow a compromise is drawn to determine the weights of the different issues on the left and on the right so that a vote for a particular candidate is in effect a vote for a block of resolutions, all of which are on balance more left or more right, as the case may be, than the block of resolutions favoured by the opposing candidate.

It is uncertain how effective a defence of democracy this is. Some factional issues might be combined and processed into a single-peaked issue in this way, but I suspect that the attempt to mobilize a left-right axis as a means of assigning a substantial part of the national income would fail; people would come to see that the assignment of income cannot effectively be subsumed under these headings, as becomes evident when a socialist government has to cope with striking firemen or with deficits in publicly owned firms. The distinction between single-peaked issues and factional issues, blurred though it may sometimes be, remains relevant in drawing the line between what voters can decide and what has to be established in a system of equity.

PRODUCTION

The instability of democracy was demonstrated in the last chapter in a model of a society where the national income appeared like manna from heaven — a society with assignment of income but without production. The question to which we now turn is whether and to what extent the gloomy assessment of the prospects for democracy derived from that model might be adjusted, and perhaps brightened a little, when we allow for the fact that the national income appears as the result of a great co-operative effort in which all workers and all of the resources of society are involved.

Production opens the possibility of a genuine capitalist equity. What was called capitalist equity in the last chapter was a contrived scheme whereby the land is divided up among citizens and each man gets to keep the manna that falls on his land. Once we take account of production, we can assign factors of production to people, identify the marginal product of each factor, and, with qualifications to be discussed, apportion the national income among people according to the marginal products of the factors they own.

The existence of a capitalist system of equity is an immediate consequence of the central proposition in economics: the docrine of the invisible hand referred to in the quotation from Adam Smith at the beginning of this chapter.[7] There is a vision or ideal of an autonomous market, of order without orders, of an economy where workers are assigned to jobs, machines are deployed, land utilized, and products distributed among people as a self interested response to prices by consumers and firms. Prices adjust, up or down, in response to scarcity or glut, ensuring that the right amount of each good is produced, with nothing wasted and no need for central direction or guidance from the public sector. It is an extraordinary, highly counter-intuitive conception rendered commonplace by familiarity among professional economists, but treated with the utmost skepticism by others to whom it is obvious that a mechanism as intricate as the economy cannot run without someone or something at the centre deciding what is to be done, how and for whom. In the branch of economics that goes by the name of the theory of general equilibrium, it is proved rigorously, subject to certain assumptions which are actually quite stringent, that an autonomous economy may exist in the sense that there is a set of prices at which, when men can buy and sell what they please at those prices, the demand for all goods just equals the supply and each man's income is fully determinate. Assumptions, qualifications and exceptions will be discussed presently. What needs to be emphasized here is that a competitive economy can apportion the national income among citizens, freeing the legislature from the need to do so, and creating the conditions for the existence of democratic government.

We must take care at this point not to claim too much. All that is asserted is that there are circumstances, more or less closely approximated by conditions in actual societies, where capitalism constitutes a perfectly and completely feasible system of equity, with an apportionment of the national income prior to and independent of the political process. Yet the correspondence between the model and the world is far from perfect. As will be discussed in detail in Chapter 5, the need for public goods and taxes, the existence of natural monopoly and the need for the legislature to specify the content of the property rights all tend to erode the feasibility of capitalist equity and to impart an element of political assignment of income in even the purest and most thoroughgoing capitalism we know. Nor need capitalism be acceptable; in fact, we shall argue in Chapter 5 that it would probably not prove acceptable to a majority of voters unless modified in important respects. As we discuss these issues, our proof of the existence of a capitalist system of equity becomes more and more hedged in with qualifications until the reader may come to wonder whether Laski's doubts about the compatibility of democracy and capitalism may not have been justified after all. But there is, as I see it, no substitute for capitalist equity. We can and do live with a mixed system, in which capitalist equity is substantially diluted with elements of other systems. We cannot dispense with capitalist equity altogether if democratic government is to be preserved.

Production also gives rise to social classes as people become differentiated in the roles they play in creating goods and services. In the 15-man example analysed in the last chapter, it was shown that there is a standing temptation for a faction to take advantage of the voting rules to direct a disproportionate share of income towards its members, but the 15 men were all alike and we had no theory of how factions arise – any eight people were as likely to combine as any other. With production comes a natural division of people according to their economic status. Farmers have interests with farmers, factory workers with factory workers, landowners with landowners, civil servants with civil servants; and the impetus to combine for economic advantage is reinforced by a tendency for one's personality, style of dress, style of speech and so on to be moulded by one's line of work so that economists, for example, are differentiated from the rest of mankind by the way they behave. The conflict of interest and personality could be so divisive that democratic government becomes unworkable, though it need not be so and is unlikely to be so if movement from class to class is reasonably fluid and if competition among the members of each class, the competition among workers for jobs and among businessmen for sales, is vigorous enough to serve as a counter-balance to the political interest they have in common.

Technology might render democratic government impossible by providing a few choice occupations and a great mass of unpleasant ones. This may have been the case in medieval Europe where the techniques of production in agriculture, the difficulty of providing protection for people and goods and the limited scope for communication over long distances required a distinction between workers and rulers, who were also fighters, or organizers of fighters, in which the condition of the rulers was so much more favourable than the condition of the workers that no legislature could assign ruling positions peacefully. One must of course, make exception for the city states of Italy, Germany and the Low Countries, where the industrial structure was entirely different from that in the countryside and where genuine democracy did flourish from time to time.

Commodities may be democratic or undemocratic. In South East Asia rice is a democratic commodity because its culture requires great care and attention to detail, most likely to be provided by independent farmers working their own land, and because rice can be stored at moderate cost, allowing the farmer to have the rice milled at a time and place of his own choosing. Sugar, by contrast, is undemocratic, because sugar cane cannot be stored after it is cut. Production has to be organized on a large tract of land and the harvesting carefully scheduled so that cane is fed into the mill at just the right moment. Thus, rice technology tends to give rise to a large class of independent holders of small amounts of property while sugar technology gives rise to a small class of owners of land and mills and a large class of landless workers.

The political propensities of commodities would depend on the technology in use. Our characterization of rice farming, for instance, took no account of irrigation. Large-scale, centrally directed irrigation requires a class of civil servants to keep the water works in repair and to allocate water among farmers. The gap between bureaucrat and farmer in an irrigated economy may be no less dangerous to democracy than the gap between mill-owner and farmer in a sugar economy. The bureaucracy could easily come to dominate society, as is alleged to have happened in many of the great Empires in the past.[8]

Oil is undemocratic for a different reason. It is undemocratic because, being worth more on today's market than the cost of extracting it from the ground, it provides a country with income that is not attached or attributable to particular people in any obvious way. It is comparable to the manna from heaven in our example in the last chapter, and sets people fighting about how income is to be assigned. North Sea oil seems to have set Scottish against English and rich against poor, the latter conflict being manifest in the question of whether oil revenue should be passed on through tax reduction or in equal amounts per man.[9] The oil of western Canada has set eastern Canadians against western Canadians, westerners wanting to sell oil at world prices, easterners wanting to tax the export of oil and to keep internal oil prices low to transfer the surplus from producers to consumers.

There is, in short, something to the notion of technical as opposed to merely economic determinism. The political propensities of the different technologies are attenuated in a diverse economy where many goods are produced and many technologies are employed at once. And I would unhesitatingly reject the extreme form of technical determinism according to which society has no choice as to the form of economic organization or the form of government once the technology is set. None the less, democratic government may be more difficult to maintain in some technologies than in others. What is to be feared is that the development of more and more complex industrial processes coupled with the continued rise in world population and the essential limits of the world's resources may be moving us into a progressively less democratic technology, into an economy with more of the characteristics of sugar than of rice.

Production also supplies the principal means for a minority to exert pressure on the majority in the legislature. If each man receives the value of the marginal products of his factors of production — and no more — then no man acting by himself can exert pressure upon the rest of the community by threatening to withdraw his labour or resources, for the rest of the community would be unaffected. But the co-ordinated withdrawal of labour or resources imposes costs upon the community, creating a situation comparable to what would happen if each of the 15 men in our example in the last chapter could, by pressing a button, eliminate, say, 20 per cent (more than his share) of the national income. Strikes and lockouts are the normal weapons in the wage-setting wherever unions and employers' associations are permitted. Similar pressures are exerted against society as a whole when doctors strike to prevent the establishment of a national health service, farmers strike for price supports or tariffs on agricultural imports, teachers, civil servants and other public sector employees strike for guaranteed employment or higher wages, or firms combine to raise prices by restricting output. The process can be pushed beyond the individual trade or industry, as in a general strike, with the object of reassigning part of the national income and some of the interesting and influential positions in society from one class to another. Any disaffected group can threaten not merely to withhold its own labour and resources, but to destroy all or part of society's means of production if its demands are not met.[10]

Society must establish rules determining when co-operative effort among firms or workers is permissible and when not. For firms, the rules take the form of anti-trust laws; for workers, they take the form of legislation specifying which workers are prohibited from striking (typically because the co-ordinated withdrawal of services would impose too large a cost on the rest of society), what steps the government may take if a strike continues beyond some specified duration or begins to be very harmful to the rest of the community, what actions by strikers are to be counted as legitimate in pursuit of their aims, and when and on what terms entry into a trade such as medicine or education may be regulated by a trade union. The establishment of the rules of economic warfare inevitably involves the legislature in the apportionment of income among trades or social classes. The extent of legislative influence is likely to be less, the closer the organization of the economy approaches the perfectly competitive ideal with all forms of monopoly eliminated.

THE DIVISION OF POWERS WITHIN GOVERNMENT

The simple model of democratic government in Chapter 2 is a two-fold abstraction. It abstracts from the context of democratic government in overlooking production, social class, bureaucracy, and other aspects of societies within which democratic governments have to function. It also abstracts from the content of democratic government in that there is no provision in the model for the prime minister, the Cabinet, members of Parliament representing constituencies, levels of government or circumstances where plurality rather than majority must be sufficient for choosing among alternative policies or candidates for office. It preserves nothing but the bare principle of majority rule.

The justification for such an enterprise is, as we have said, that the political consequences of economic policy are frequently overlooked and may be most effectively studied within a model where links are prominently displayed. We have, in effect, traded realism for emphasis. The model of democracy focuses directly on the feature responsible for the constraint upon economic arrangements. Our procedure is to test alternative economic institutions and policies for their effects in strengthening or weakening democracy with reference to this feature alone, on the working assumption that constraints upon economic arrangements derived from the simple model of majority rule would not be materially affected if we took account, for instance, of the fact that citizens influence the decisions of the legislature indirectly through election of members of Parliament. The simple model is tractable and provides insights into connections between economy and government that might be overlooked without its aid. Whether the model really is adequate for its purpose is a matter for the reader to decide in the light of the analysis throughout the book. No model can be ruled out because of its simplicity, and there is no contradiction between treating the preservations of actual democratic government as an objective and employing a pathetically simple model of democracy in our analysis.

It is arguable, however, that in focusing upon the simple model of majority rule we have inadvertently ignored many of the supports and defences of actual democratic governments in the countries where they are to be found. The prospects for democracy may not be as bleak as the simple model would suggest. In particular, in abstracting from the content of democratic government, we have eliminated the checks and balances among levels of government upon which the stability of democratic government is traditionally believed to depend. A proper division of powers among legislature, executive and judiciary is commonly thought of as a defence against the emergence of dictatorship. Federal government has been advocated as a means to control the mischief of faction in each level of government through the influence of other factions at other levels of government. These defences of democracy cannot even be discussed within the context of the model we have designed.

The importance of this omission depends critically on how the theory of checks and balances is interpreted. Remember that the subject of this book is the *economic* prerequisite to democracy, a necessary but not necessarily sufficient condition. The form of the argument is that you cannot have democratic government unless certain economic prerequisites are satisfied. The reverse is not claimed at all. Democracy may require the economic prerequisite and more besides. Hence there is no fundamental contradiction between the theory of checks and balances and the analysis of this book as long as a proper division of powers is also thought of as a necessary but not sufficient condition for democracy. Only if a proper division of powers were alleged to be sufficient for democratic government — an extreme position, according to which no economic or social conditions would matter as long as the organization of government is satisfactory — would the analysis in this book be undermined. Otherwise there is no logical barrier to accepting the analysis of this book and the theory of checks and balances as well. It would of course be desirable to encompass both in a broader model of democratic government.

THE CIVIL SERVICE

So compelling is the vision of a self regulating economy that one sometimes forgets that society needs regulation at all. Adam Smith, David Ricardo and many other classical economists discussed the apportionment of income among landowners, capitalists and workers, ignoring — at least until the chapter on public finance — the motives, standard of remuneration and sometimes the very existence of the army, the police, the judiciary and the civil service. Marx's conception of the government as the passive instrument of the capitalist class has dominated socialist thought to such an extent that it was possible for an ex-communist to startle his former colleagues a few years ago with the revelation that the party and the civil service in communist countries constitute a new class.[11] Only recently has the notion of a bureaucracy with interests of its own — interests that are neither more nor less likely to coincide with the public interest than are the interests of farmers, doctors, the unemployed or the executives of large corporations — been taken seriously within the science of economics.[12] Note that the term 'bureaucracy.' is used here in a broad sense to refer to the public service as a whole: the prime minister, members of Parliament, the army, the civil service proper and top management in public enterprises.

Bureaucracy carries special prizes which are difficult for a democratic society to assign particular people. Suppose, returning to our 15-man example, that the manna falling from heaven is not a perfectly divisible stuff to be assigned in any manner whatsoever, but falls instead in 15 boxes, five containing $30,000, five containing $20,000 and five containing $10,000. Each man may receive one and only one box, and there is no mechanism for compelling someone who receives a box containing $30,000 to share his good fortune with his poorer neighbours. Bureaucracy is like that. It creates positions, limited in number, that are more attractive than any alternative open to the occupants. The source of the attractiveness of senior positions may be power, the feeling that one is personally influencing events, the possibility of being remembered in the history books, prestige among one's associates, or the intrinsic interest of the job. Frequently, the nature of a post requires, or is alleged to require, an income higher than what the occupant would be prepared to accept. It is considered prudent to pay judges well because a dishonest judge may impose a great cost on society and because the risk of a judge being dishonest is reduced when he is well paid. Diplomats have to live in a style befitting the dignity of their countries. Senior civil servants acquire contacts that prove valuable should they choose to leave the service.

Democratic societies try to design systems of equity for hiring and promoting civil servants. Wherever possible, civil servants are paid what they might earn in comparable jobs in the private sector. The democracies of ancient Greece and medieval Italy went farther. It was thought to be an essential feature of democracy that high office be assigned by lot, so that each citizen over his lifetime had an equal chance at the perquisites of office.[13] One way or another, democracies attempt to limit the number and value of posts that must be politically assigned, to arrange for more boxes with $20,000 and fewer boxes with $30,000 or $10,000, or to extract some of the extra income from the large boxes. The attempt is never altogether successful. The degree of success depends, in part, on the size of the bureaucracy and the extent of its power.

The larger the bureaucracy, the more powerful it becomes, and the greater is the danger of its choosing to dispense with democracy and run society in its own interest. One sees this process pushed to bizarre extremes in the pyramids of Egypt or the great temples of Angkor Wat, where the stylized face of the king, repeated again and again in stone, looks down at you from every direction. Indeed, considering that the bureaucracy typically has a monopoly of weapons and of the means of communication, the surprising fact is not that the bureaucracy frequently gets the upper hand, but that it ever fails to do so. In the Middle Ages, there were rudimentary parliaments in all the major countries of Europe. Of these, only one — the Parliament of England — survived the Renaissance to serve as the model for democratic government in the modern world. A major historian[14] has attributed this anomaly to the success of the Norman and Angevin kings in extending their rule over the whole of England at a time before the revival of learning permitted the establishment of a proper judicial and administrative service. Authority had to be delegated to the regional nobility and local squires, whose power could not be subsequently withdrawn, but could only be exercised at the centre through a legislature, and came to be shared with the great mass of people in the nineteenth and early twentieth centuries.

As we shall argue at some length in Chapters 4 and 5, the preservation of democratic government requires that the power of the bureaucracy, the number of men on the government payroll and the range of authority of the civil service over the economy be kept within bounds. Where to draw the line is difficult to say, though Canada and the United States are presumably on one side while China and the Soviet Union appear to be well on the other. Even when the army and civil service can be kept entirely under the thumb of the legislature, the power they inevitably wield serves as a focus of rivalry among social groups, the more so, the greater the extent of that power, the greater the capacity of the bureaucracy to redirect income from one industry or region to another, and the more jobs at the government's disposal. The influence of the bureaucracy may become too great a prize for the party in office to risk losing at the ballot box; there may, quite simply, be too much at stake in the election for the democratic process to continue.

SOCIAL CLASS

The indeterminacy of the composition of the majority faction in our 15-man example is, in a sense, instructive because it serves to emphasize that the voting rules themselves draw forth factions, regardless of the intentions of the voters. The rules exert a pressure upon the community, causing it to split along whatever potential lines of division are already there. Any differentiation may serve as a badge by which one's faction is identified. Race is the most durable and most effective badge, which is why there are so few multiracial democracies, the main exceptions being countries like the United States, where one race is so numerically dominant that it has nothing to fear from the granting of political rights to others.[15] Religion can be just as effective, though it need not be so. Religious tolerance and the insistence that a man's belief is his own personal affair with no public significance is the counterpart of a system of equity in the economic sphere. Religion served as a political badge in British India on the eve of Independence as Hindus and Muslims made it clear they were not prepared to share the same society. Language is the axis of division in Belgium, where a clear line has been drawn between French and Flemish parts of the country, and in Canada, where the proportion of the French-speaking minority in the country as a whole is just about equal to the proportion of the English-speaking minority in the Province of Quebec and the threat of separation of Quebec hangs over every move in economic or political affairs. Geography itself may acquire political significance, especially where regional solidarity is reinforced by economics, religion or social characteristics. Finally, there is the class structure emerging from the economy, the division rich and poor (in so far as these can be treated as characteristics of people prior to the political process), or the conflict among businessmen, civil servants and trade unions as rival political elites, each seeking to enhance its sphere of influence and to develop a following among the voters at large – a conflict particularly evident in contemporary Britain and, with even greater force if we omit trade unions, in Malaysia, where the business-civil service axis reinforces a religious and ethnic cleavage.

The instability of democracy is as much a cause as a consequence of rivalry among classes of voters. Differences of one sort or another are inevitable, but political arrangements determine if they will be divisive. Whether the king be Catholic or Protestant was of the greatest significance in Tudor and Stuart England. Whether the president be Catholic or Protestant was relatively unimportant in the United States in the 1960s. Religious, linguistic or racial loyalties may be more or less divisive to a society depending on the extent and solidity of the system of equity in force. If the system of equity is strong, if everyone agrees that the national income is to be divided equally among citizens and positions of authority allocated by lot; or, alternatively, if property rights are treated as inviolate and the role of government is pared down to the irreducible minimum advocated by many conservative thinkers, then there is little to be gained by emphasizing solidarity with others who share one's race, language or religion. But where advancement in society, high incomes and positions of authority are in the gift of the legislature, it becomes advantageous for members of the same race, language or religion to vote as a block within a majority coalition or to develop a capacity to sabotage the economy and make life miserable for everyone else to provide the legislature with an incentive to accede to its demands. It is discovered that East is East and West is West, that there is a white man's burden, that black is beautiful, or that workers of the world should unite. The sentiment of loyalty that might otherwise be directed to society as a whole becomes more narrowly focused on one's church, ethnic association, region or trade union.

Two other propositions, which are really two sides of the same coin, follow almost as corollaries to the foregoing: that political assignment of incomes can be pushed farther in a homogeneous society than in a plural society, and that democracy can be maintained in a plural society only through a system of equity that leaves a bare minimum of assignment to the legislature. The religious, linguistic and cultural homogeneity of the Scandinavian countries may explain why they have been able to proceed as far as they have with socialism without, at the same time, destroying democracy. A socialist Switzerland is inconceivable (though, I must confess, things inconceivable to academic economists do sometimes happen). The internal contradiction in political assignment of incomes in a plural society may be at the root of recent developments in Quebec. As long as the federal and provincial governments played a relatively small role in economic affairs, it was possible for French and English communities to go their own ways; to live, in the words of the title of a famous novel, as 'two solitudes'. As the public sector grew; as government exercised an ever larger influence on the geography of investment; as there developed elaborate transfer mechanisms in which the federal government collected taxes to be passed on in the form of grants to the provinces; and with the introduction of public health insurance, public support of higher education and research, and the old age pension, there arose innumerable opportunities for conflict of interest between the French and English communities – conflict that has now erupted in an expressed desire on the part of a substantial minority of French Canadians for a separate state in Quebec.

There is possibly another side to social class that has been much emphasized by political scientists and that may require modification of our analysis. Just as economists see an invisible hand that guides the self-interested and unco-ordinated actions of consumers and firms to a common good, so political scientists have a notion of a political equilibrium achieved through the interaction of a multitude of pressure groups, with the extreme demands of each moderated and contained by the influence of the rest. A distinction is made between cross-cutting and reinforcing cleavages, the former supportive and the latter detrimental to democracy.[16] Religion and language are reinforcing cleavages in Quebec because French can, for the most part, be identified with Catholicism and English can, for the most part, be identified with Protestantism. Religion and wealth, on the other hand, are cross-cutting cleavages because, though Protestants may, on average, be better off, there are significant numbers of rich Catholics and poor Protestants.

The theory that pressure groups interact to yield a political equilibrium is a difficult theory to assess. There is a sense in which it has to be true: pressure groups are a common feature in all the democracies we know. But it is also true that democracies collapse from time to time, and the real question is whether and to what extent we can look upon political assignment of income with equanimity, trusting to countervailing power among social groups to keep democracy on an even keel. To the best of my knowledge, there has as yet been devised no formal theory of the interaction of pressure groups comparable to the theory of general equilibrium in economics in which the interaction of consumers and firms is proved on certain assumptions to yield a determinate structure of output and assignment of the national income. Confidence in the existence of a political equilibrium rests on gut feelings, hunches and experience of political activity.

FRANCHISE

There is a simple defence of the system of equity we have not yet considered. The system of equity has at times been protected by not enfranchising those who may be expected to use their votes to violate its rules. It is a dangerous expedient because the unenfranchised may become enemies of the state and because, in modern times at least, the principle of equality has so strong a hold on our minds that no system of equity is likely to win assent, even of a favoured minority, if the principle of equality is violated. None the less, democracy grew up under limited franchise, and it is at least arguable that the economic conditions for universal franchise have been achieved only in this century.

We are inclined to look upon the gradual extension of suffrage as analogous to moral progress and in a strictly political context. The history of the great reform bills in nineteenth and early twentieth-century England is thought of as comparable to the growth of science or the development of mass production. We do things better now because we know better, and if the people in 1800 had the same ideals as we do they would have established universal suffrage on the spot. There is another way of looking at that development. Take as a premise that, until well into the nineteenth century, the preservation of individual liberty and the maintenance of Parliament were dependent upon a system of equity based on private property in an economy with great disparities of wealth and an enormous gulf between upper and lower classes, for no other system of equity was compatible with the technology in use. Take as a second premise that the poor, if enfranchised, would have voted to expropriate the rich, eliminating the only system of equity available at the time. It follows that men who might have wished for democracy with universal suffrage would have had to make do with limited suffrage if democracy were to be maintained at all. Aristotle recognized this problem and recommended a system of voting in which the votes of the rich were more heavily weighted than the votes of the poor.[17] The problem plagued the city states of the ancient world and medieval Europe. It was recognized by Oliver Cromwell in his opposition to universal suffrage in England.[18] It explains why the classical economists were often opposed to universal suffrage.[19]

What changed in the course of the nineteenth century was not so much the community's values as the underlying conditions in the economy. On the one hand, general prosperity gave the average man a stake in society and an incentive to uphold existing economic arrangements. On the other hand, there evolved relatively harmless methods of redistribution. Redistribution in the eighteenth century could not have been other than a great scramble of the poor to take what they could from the rich, a process that would surely have eliminated the incentive to invest or to develop new methods of production. Techniques of administration have since then advanced to the point where redistribution, in the form of the old age pension, the progressive income tax, food stamps and so on, is an orderly process, preserving enough of the advantages of wealth that the incentive to work, save and innovate is maintained and the willingness to abide by the rule of the majority is not destroyed.

It is doubtful whether anything short of universal franchise can be preserved under present conditions. There would appear to be no middle ground between democracy with universal franchise and dictatorship administered by the army or by a political party that admits no effective opposition. Yet democracy was nurtured in ancient Greece and once again in England under a suffrage that was, at first, restricted, but that could be extended by degrees until it became universal.

POLITICAL PARTIES

We abstract from political parties in our 15-man example in Chapter 2 and in our analysis of equity under socialism and capitalism later on in the book. We do so because we cannot study everything at once, because a model with only an economy and a legislature is sufficient to display the connection between them, and because the moral of the story — that democratic government can be maintained only if there are severe constraints on the extent to which the democratic process is used to apportion income among citizens — is reinforced when political parties are taken into account.

Political parties compound and magnify the problem of faction in two important respects. First, as permanent ongoing institutions, they can play the role of catalyst around which interest groups, based on language, religion, geography or economic considerations, can form for the purpose of constituting a permanent majority in the legislature. Second, as potential governments, they magnify the advantages of being in the majority. If the Eastern party forms the government, it is not only in a position to pass legislation favouring the economic interests of easterners, but it can staff the senior ranks of the civil service with easterners to see to it that the laws are administered to the easterners' advantage.

How political parties serve as catalyst and instrument of faction depends, in part, on the voting rules in force. Proportional representation is alleged to foster small parties with special interests that have to be reconciled within the legislature; there could be a truckers' party, a doctors' party or an economists' party if truckers', doctors' or econo-mists' concern for the problems of their profession takes precedence over their concern as citizens for broader aspects of public policy. A system such as we have in Canada, the United States and the United Kingdom, with one representative per constituency, emphasizes geography rather than occupation, religion or language, except where an occupation, religion or language is geographically concentrated; and it requires the diverse interests in a majority coalition to be reconciled before, rather than after, the election. But whatever the system of representation, one would expect that the incentive for political parties seeking office to coalesce and polarize around special interests would increase together with the extent of political influence in the assignment of the national income.

Difficulties with political assignment of income in a democracy are compounded by the peculiar dynamics of rivalry among political parties seeking office. The role of the political party in representing a coalition of interest groups or social classes — as a party must do if it is to be elected — conflicts with its role in governing the country. Not infre-quently, voters are confronted with a choice between a party competent to govern but opposed to policies they desire, and a less competent party favourably disposed to their special concerns. Such a choice is alleged to have confronted the voters in the Quebec election of 1976, when a federalist majority in the population had to choose between an apparently more competent separatist party and an apparently less competent federalist party. The voters chose competence in that case, but there are other cases where incompetent or unpopular leaders become irremovable for long periods of time because the majority would not tolerate the policy of the opposition. The more polarized are the political parties over the issues, the more costly it becomes to abandon a political party because of its lack of fitness to govern, and the more likely it becomes that the decline of democracy will be assisted by the decline of the quality of its leaders.

Vote-splitting among political parties with similar programmes may lead to a misrepresentation of the will of the majority of the electorate. If two parties favour policy A while only one favours policy B, the party favouring B may win a majority of the seats in the legislature because it wins more votes than either of the other parties individually, though not more than the two combined. Alternatively, fear of the growth of one extreme may provoke voters to support the opposite extreme, at the expense of a centre position preferred by most voters. A process of this kind may account, in part, for the decay of the Weimar Republic. Voters who would really prefer the continuance of the Republic may have found themselves voting for Nazis or Communists to ensure the defeat of the other, seen as the greater evil.

The resilience of democracy in the face of these difficulties may come to depend on the relative strengths of parochial and national loyalities. Does the farmer vote for the farmers' party or for a broad party, like Labour, Liberal or Conservative, that might subordinate the interest of farmers to other considerations of foreign or domestic affairs? Does the Welshman in Britain vote for a party specifically and exclusively concerned with Welsh interests, or does he vote for another party with a wider range of concern? To what extent can a member of Parliament be counted upon to put the interest of the nation as he sees it ahead of the immediate interests of his constituents? Democracy may depend on having members of Parliament – and citizens disposed to elect such members of Parliament – whose first loyalty is to the nation as a whole. The importance of equity in this context is that political loyalty itself may be a consequence of economic arrangements. If the degree of feasibility of equity is high and political assignment is pared down to the point where the major part of each man's income is determined prior to and independently of decisions in the legislature, then the cost of loyalty to one's nation, as opposed to one's region or special interest group, is not excessive. Attenuate the system of equity, allow large amounts of income to be assigned by the legislature, and a rivalry among regions or economic classes is created automatically, together with a sectional loyalty that detracts from one's allegiance to the nation as a whole.

THE DISINTEGRATION OF DEMOCRACY

Within our 15-man example, we could predict that democracy without a system of equity was not viable, but we could not predict the manner of its decline. After endless wrangling over the assignment of income, with coalitions forming and dissolving, with threats and counter-threats giving way to occasional violence, and with the national income unassigned for long periods of time because no agreement could be reached as to how shares are to be chosen, our 15 men may become so disenchanted with democracy that they appoint a sovereign. Alternatively, an eight-man coalition may succeed in reserving a disproportionate share of the national income for itself, but only at the cost of generating evergreater hostility on the part of the seven dispossessed, who must ultimately be dealt with by force. It is unlikely that a democracy can last for long when a bare majority has to compel an unwilling minority to accept the rules. Suspicious of one another, and each fearing the formation of a new majority coalition from which he might be excluded, the eight may come to prefer the rule of a dictator who, being one of them, is trusted to respect their privileges over the seven, and to employ force to keep the seven in their place. The seven themselves may rebel to establish a dictatorship of the proletariate or a monarch to look after the religious, linguistic, geographic or economic class to which they belong. There is, of course, the possibility that, after much bickering, the 15, or a large majority of them, will settle upon a method of assigning incomes and come to an understanding that the method will be respected in perpetuity, as a means of reducing conflict to the point where democracy can continue for such matters as the choice of leaders, dealings with other tribes and changes in the law. An agreement or understanding of this kind is precisely what we mean by a system of equity, and our prediction about the instability of democracy is, of course, a conditional prediction of what will happen if such an agreement cannot be reached.

The instability of democracy without equity is the same, but the manner of its decline is even less predictable when we pass from the small, simple society in which equity is defined to actual democratic societies with production, social classes, representative government, political parties and all of the other complexities assumed away to make our story convincing. Lacking a comprehensive model of democratic government, I can only remind the reader of the many cases where democracy has disintegrated or failed to take root and suggest that the absence of a system of equity or its gradual disintegration was a contributing factor.

The immediate cost of the attenuation of equity is the disorganization as each class and pressure group demonstrates its capacity to disrupt society if its interests are not taken into account. In principle, threats could be exercised silently and costlessly, with each party proving its capacity for mischief without actually engaging in mischief, and the legislature acting with due regard for the strength of the different groups affected in every vote. This does not happen in practice because, as we know from industrial disputes, threats must occasionally be exercised to be believable and, more important, because the equilibrium in conflicts among pressure groups is so ill-defined that parties are unlikely to accept an outcome without a trial of strength. The cost of administering democracy rises in stages. At a minimum, there are the ordinary costs of conducting elections, running pressure groups, influencing public opinion, and petitioning the government to favour this or that cause, interest or firm, together with the distortion in economic and political life when the government is overly influenced by group demands. Costs rise sharply when economic weapons are used to influence the outcome of elections, as in the UK miners' strike of 1974. Economic warfare can escalate to rioting, destruction of property, intimidation of members of the opposing factions, and attacks on unsympathetic political leaders. How far this process is allowed to proceed would depend in part on how much is believed to be at stake and on the degree of support the government can command in suppressing what is thought of as antisocial behaviour. Faced with mounting extra-parliamentary opposition, and apprehensive about what might happen to members of the ruling party and their supporters in the event of an opposition victory, the ruling party is ever more tempted to employ the power of government illegally against its opponents, whose antagonism increases accordingly.

As the stakes of office escalate and pressure groups become progressively more desperate and more willing to sabotage the economy or to commit violence to achieve their aims, there develops a tendency in the electorate to polarize around religious, linguistic, geographic or economic lines. Leaders of contending factions begin to contemplate the replacement of democratic government, if only as a means of forestalling *coup d'état* by an opposing faction. At that point, it may make little difference whether democracy comes to an end through the election of a leader expected to assume dictatorial powers, as in the demise of the Weimar Repulic, or by *coup d'état,* as in Chile, Indonesia, the Bolshevik Revolution and numerous military takeovers throughout the world.

To say that rivalry among social groups can be contained and its most destructive manifestations prevented by a strong system of equity is almost tautological; people will not fight if they can agree without fighting. But there is more to it than that. As we show in detail in the final chapter of this book, the system of equity can be strengthened or attenuated by economic policies in ways that may not be anticipated when these policies are adopted.

4

Equality and Socialism

. . . in the socialist community, the necessity of acting in common must raise the question of how to act in common. It will be necessary to decide how to form . . . the will of the people. Even if we overlooked the fact that there can be no administration of goods which is not administration of men . . . we should still have to ask who is to administer the goods and direct the productive processes, and on what principles . . . All historical attempts to realize the socialist ideal of society have a most pronounced authoritarian character.

Ludwig von Mises[1]

. . . the real danger of socialism is the bureaucratization of economic life . . . .

Oskar Lange[2]

The argument, so far, can be summarized in a few simple propositions. An actual or proposed method of assigning incomes and other advantages to citizens is said to conform to a system of equity if it is feasible in the sense of being prior to and independent of the political process, so that the government need not step in to say who gets what, and if it is acceptable in the sense that no majority has an incentive to replace the method of assignment by another system of equity or by direct political assignment. The central proposition of the book, developed in Chapter 2 and extended in Chapter 3, is that democracy requires a system of equity because the legislature cannot assign incomes without at the same time destroying the consensus required for the preservation of democratic government. The proposition is less radical than it may first appear, for assignment is interpreted in a special sense that does not preclude redistribution of income as ordinarily understood. The distinction is that redistribution reduces the gap between rich and poor but preserves the ordering, so that if Mr A were better off than Mr B before redistribution he would continue to be so afterward, while reassignment of income interchanges people on the scale of rich and poor. Redistribution may actually strengthen democratic government by enhancing the acceptability of the system of equity in force. It was also shown that perfect competition as described in textbooks of economics is entirely and completely feasible as a system of equity, though it may be unacceptable if substantial numbers of people turn out to be poor. And, as became evident in our discussion of bureaucracy, the ideal of a perfectly and completely feasible system of equity in which incomes are established with no influence whatsoever from the political arena is unattainable in practice. The real question is whether any known system of industrial organization contains an assignment mechanism sufficiently independent of the political arena to allow democratic government to proceed.

It is to this question that we now turn, and our focus is henceforth less political and more economic. The argument from here on can be summarized in four propositions: (1) that neither full and complete equality nor socialism, defined as public ownership of the means of production, will do as a system of equity; (2) that capitalism as we know it (as distinct from the textbook model of perfect competition) contains a weak system of equity which is only just feasible; (3) that the acceptability of capitalism probably depends on the fact that there is no alternative method of economic organization consistent with democracy and conducive to economic growth; and (4) that the capitalist system of equity may be shored up by judicious choice of economic policy or attenuated if economic policy is unfavourable. These propositions are examined in the three remaining chapters of the book.

EQUALITY

Equality would, I think, be the leading candidate for a system of equity in a small society where the income falls like manna from heaven, may be plucked off trees, or accrues from co-operative effort as in a hunt where no man's marginal contribution can be identified for the assignment of his share. But it is out of the question as a system of equity in a modern industrial economy because it would destroy incentives and is logically inconsistent with the minimal degree of hierarchy an industrial society requires.

Full equality would be unacceptable because it would destroy the incentive to work, save or educate oneself, and would thereby cause the national income to fall well below what would be possible if a degree of inequality were allowed. It is, in a three-person economy, as though incomes of 30 for Mr A, 20 for Mr B and 10 for Mr C could be equalized only if all three incomes were reduced to 5. If incomes are to be equal today, I have no motive to work longer hours or to exert myself more on the job than the minimum society can enforce, for extra effort on my part accrues to society as a whole and not to me. If incomes are to be equalized tomorrow, I have no motive to save or to educate myself.

In work, saving and education, it is in each man's interest to be a free rider, to exploit the efforts of others without contributing himself. But as there are no free rides for society as a whole, the net effect of an economic organization that gives each man the incentive to act as a free rider is the impoverishment of the whole. A society where all incomes are equal by law will be a poor society if it can subsist at all. Understanding this, citizens reject the principle of full and complete equality in favour of a method of assignment more conducive to prosperity and economic growth.

The ideal of equality may be defended against this line of argument on either of two grounds: (1) that full and complete equality is a caricature of what people really desire under the name of equality; and (2) that efficiency and equality can be made compatible if each man is compelled to do his share of the work. The first defence would emphasize that the call for equality is a call to reduce the gross disparities in income, opportunity, and especially inherited wealth in our society, without at the same time eliminating the reward for work, skill, saving or education. Admittedly, there may be some loss of income in the process, but a moderate loss attendant on a reasonable degree of equalization may be acceptable, though the greater loss in complete equalization would not. I have no objection to this line of reasoning *per se*. The assertion that full and complete equality would not be acceptable as a system of equity is not a denial of the validity of equality as an ideal, or a blanket objection to proposals for alleviating poverty and reducing the gap between rich and poor, or a justification for the present distribution of income. It is no more than the assertion that, as full and complete equality is unattainable or undesirable, a different principle altogether is required to assign the high incomes and low incomes, the senior positions and junior positions, that remain when no greater degree of equality can be attained or equalization of incomes has been pushed as far as the majority of voters is prepared to go. I am much less sympathetic to the second defence, for men cannot be compelled to work, save or educate themselves without someone to do the compelling; and it is, as a rule, beyond the capacity of the organization of society to maintain equality between the compeller and the compelled.

Regardless of its acceptability, full equality among citizens would be infeasible as a system of equity because, in contrast to a hunting and fishing community where full equality may really be possible, a modern industrial society cannot operate without a certain minimum of hierarchy. There can only be one prime minister, a few hundred members of Parliament, a limited number of top civil servants and senior corporation executives, a modest number of professional people; and somebody has got to collect the rubbish, dig the coal, and drive the trucks. The attractiveness of certain jobs and the onerousness of others can, to some extent, be compensated with income, as for instance where particularly dangerous jobs are correspondingly well paid. But I can conceive of no system of remuneration that would leave an ambitious man indifferent between being prime minister and being a truck driver, or would remove all incentive to rise in the hierarchy. This is partly because the temptation to be on top, to compel rather than to be compelled, is too great, and partly because the men on top inevitably manage to take care of themselves pretty well, both financially and in the perquisites of office. It is probably more than can be expected of people to suppose that those who occupy the senior positions in society will not, one way or another, arrange for themselves to have material advantages not shared by the rest of the population. I know of no societies where this is not so.

There may even be a trade-off between inequality of income and inequality of status. The point is not that inequality of status necessarily hurts more when incomes are equalized, though this may be the case. It is that a society that relies less on income differentials as a goad to economic performance would have to rely more on hierarchy and command. The creation and maintenance of a society where incomes are equal would necessarily require an extension of the size and power of the civil service and a ranking of all workers in a single chain of command. The civil service would, in the end, become the only channel of advancement; the drive to command rather than to be commanded would be stronger; and, all things considered, the inequalities among people and the political tensions they entail are not likely to be less.

SOCIALISM

Socialism is a word with many meanings. A man may call himself a socialist though all he intends in practice is that the income tax should be progressive and steps should be taken to abolish serious poverty where it occurs. We are employing a much stronger definition. An economy is socialist for the purposes of this discussion if the means of production are owned by the state and production is supervised by a planning commission, more or less as is done in Eastern Europe and the USSR.

The problem at hand is that raised in the quotations from Laski and Hayek at the beginning of Chapter 1. We wish to determine whether a country with a socialist economy can have a democratic form of government. Our analysis of equity in Chapters 2 and 3 provides some insight as to what is required of the economy if democracy is to be sustained. Democracy requires the economy to make the major assignment of income and other advantages, determining who shall be rich and who shall be poor, who is to command and who is to be commanded – a task that the legislature can never perform for itself. Social democracy is possible if a socialist economy can perform that task, and it is impossible otherwise. I shall argue that there can be no socialist system of equity; and that the establishment of socialism – defined as nothing less than the complete ownership of the means of production by the state – would sooner or later split voters into factions with interests so sharply opposed that democratic government could not be maintained.

The style of the argument is proof by contradiction, though the argument itself is informal. We imagine a socialist system of equity, work out what its character would have to be, and show that it cannot be realized in practice. The demonstration focuses upon the task of the planner and on the manner of his appointment by the legislature. To divest itself of the responsibility for the assignment of income, the legislature would have to supply the planner, once and for all, with a set of instructions on how to direct the economy – what to produce, how to set prices and wages, and how to assign people to slots in the hierarchy. It would also be necessary for the legislature to appoint the planner, without, at the same time, having to assign incomes indirectly through its choice among candidates who can be expected to favour different industries, regions or social classes. Much depends upon the criterion that the planner is expected to adopt. If the criterion is exact and comprehensive, then perhaps the planner can direct the economy like a mathematician solving a complex problem. We shall show that the only more or less acceptable criteria are vague in their implications, so that the planner must exercise his own judgement on a wide range of issues where the assignment of income depends critically on what he decides to do; and the legislature, unwilling or unable to tolerate an independent authority over the economy, would have to become involved.

We shall develop this argument in some detail, but before doing so we consider an objection the reader might be inclined to raise, an objection related in a general way to a point already discussed in Chapter 2. We are about to argue that social democracy is impossible because it forces the assignment of income into the legislature. It might well be objected that the assignment of income is in the legislature already, that political assignment can never be avoided in any society, democratic or otherwise, and that, if assignment in the legislature renders democratic socialism impossible, it must render democratic capitalism impossible as well. The critic can appeal to a mass of evidence that legislatures do succeed in reaching agreements affecting the incomes of their constituents. Bargains are struck, and politicians manage to split the difference in apparently irreconcilable disputes. Perhaps the same mysterious process that works on a small scale in wage-setting between union and management can be made to work on a large scale in the organization of the economy under socialism.

In defence against this line of attack, I would appeal to the distinction between an incomplete system of equity and the absence of a system of equity. Of course, legislators bargain. Democratic government requires that they be able to do so. But there is an essential difference between bargaining in a context where the amount at stake is small relative to the incomes of the parties concerned because the bulk of one's income is determined in the private sector independently of the political arena, and decision-making in a legislature where the whole of one's income and status is at stake. The argument that there is no socialist system of equity is an argument that *all*, or almost all, assignment is forced into the legislature. That argument is not weakened significantly by the fact that *part* of income is assigned by the legislature in every democratic society we know. The difference between assignment by the legislature in capitalist countries and in socialist countries, is, admittedly, a difference in amount rather than in kind, but the difference is none the less sufficient to make democracy viable in one case and inviable in the other. One can, by the same token, reject evidence on bargaining in industrial disputes as irrelevant to the question of whether social democracy is possible, for bargaining is feasible as a means of apportioning income among people only when the amount at stake is moderate, when the bulk of the incomes of all parties is determined elsewhere, and when the cost to all parties of not reaching an agreement is high by comparison with the amount at stake in the bargaining process.

Evidence on the experience of socialist countries is much more relevant and in complete conformity with what the analysis in this chapter would lead us to expect. To the best of my knowledge, no state at once socialist and democratic has ever been observed. Many states have been called social democratic, but in each case the word 'socialism' or the word 'democracy' has had a meaning different from that used here. In Western Europe, socialism refers to the welfare state, a degree of state ownership of industry and perhaps the intention to extend state ownership eventually. In Eastern Europe, on the other hand, the means of production are owned almost entirely by the state, but the word 'democracy' is used to describe one-party states which, whatever their virtues, are not democracies as defined in this book.

A system of equity is a mechanism for assigning incomes independently of the legislature. Capitalism contains a system of equity if and in so far as incomes can be assigned as a by-product of competition among privately owned firms. Socialism substitutes planning for property. The existence of a socialist system of equity must therefore depend on whether the planner can maintain an independence from the legislature not appreciably less than that maintained between the private sector and the legislature in a capitalist economy. In dealing with this question, we shall speak of the planner as a person, but the argument applies equally to a planning commission or a more complex instrument of control.

Consider the powers of the planner in a socialist economy. The planner must decide what to produce. He must set prices of all goods. He must set wages in all occupations and in every region of the country. He must assign workers to slots in a great hierarchy comprising the whole workforce of the nation. He must decide who is to be promoted. He must choose investment projects, and, in doing so, must determine which regions of the country are to expand and which are to contract. He must decide when industrial establishments are to be shut down because they are no longer socially desirable. He must design and administer a system of incentives so that workers up and down the hierarchy are led by self-interest or by fear to do what is best for the nation. And because the profit motive is largely, though not entirely, eliminated, the incentives in a socialist economy become, like the incentives in the civil service or the public school system of a capitalist economy, less dependent than incentives in the private sector on automatic monetary reward for correct behaviour, and more dependent on the fear of dismissal for unsatisfactory performances or the desire to improve one's prospects for promotion by cultivating the goodwill of one's supervisor. But the planner's power over the labour force in a socialist economy is substantially greater than the government's power over the civil service in a capitalist economy, because there is no private sector as a safety-valve for the insubordinate, for someone who feels that his income is too low, or for someone passed over for promotion by a less competent rival. A worker who has run afoul of the socialist hierarchy remains at its mercy and must accept whatever employment and remuneration the state chooses to provide. The authority of the planner over incomes and careers of workers throughout the economy is augmented still further by the intrinsic difficulty of the planning problem. Without genuine competition among firms, it is often difficult to say with assurance what ought to be produced and whether workers and managers have behaved correctly, except where specific orders have to be obeyed.

The existence of a socialist system of equity depends on whether these formidable powers of the planner can be de-contaminated through a general rule supplied by the legislature for the planner to follow in day-to-day decision-making. The question is whether a middle ground can be discovered between giving so much power to the planner that he replaces the legislature as the ruler of the state, and reserving so much of the authority over the economy for the legislature that there remains no other place where income and other advantages may be assigned.

The planner in a dictatorship manages the economy according to the wishes of the dictator, and the economy can be rearranged when the dictator changes his mind. In a democracy where, as we have shown, the legislature must not involve itself in the assignment of incomes, the planner must be supplied with a criterion that is acceptable to a majority of voters and expected to hold for a long period of time. The planner might be told to make the national income as large as possible on the understanding that the resulting income is divided equally among all citizens, or to direct the employment of resources and to assign incomes to people so as to maximize the national income regardless of the consequences for the distribution of income, or to follow a mixed rule that draws a balance between the maximization of national income and the equalization of incomes among citizens. We shall examine these criteria in turn.

As has already been shown in our discussion of equality, the first of these criteria is intrinsically not feasible (because positions in a hierarchy cannot be assigned equally, and because hierarchy is particularly important in a socialist state) and would, in any case, be unacceptable because the loss of potential output through the killing of incentives is too great. The second is feasible enough but, I should imagine, unacceptable to the poorer half of the community who, even under a capitalist system, insist that the distribution of income be modified in their favour. The third, the only serious candidate, is really a family of criteria, each member of which corresponds to a separate weighting of total income and equality on a common scale.

The weighting of efficiency and equality in the objective function of a socialist planner is analogous to the choice of progressivity in the income tax, where a greater progressivity results in a somewhat smaller pie (a lower total national income because of the disincentive effect of the tax) and a more equal slicing of the pie. Among weightings, the most favourable to the poor is the 'maximin principle', which focuses exclusively on the worst off person in society; the planner would direct the economy so as to make the worst off person as well off as he can be under the circumstances.[3] The maximin principle does not require income to be divided equally among all citizens, for the worst off person may be better off if some degree of inequality is allowed. If, to return to an example used above, the only way to equalize incomes among Mr A, Mr B and Mr C is to reduce incomes of 30, 20 and 10 respectively to 5, 5 and 5, the maximin principle would reject the change despite the greater equality. A broader class of weightings of efficiency and equality, of which the maximin principle is a special and limiting case, is 'utilitarianism'. Utilitarianism is a venerable doctrine with many variants, but we may think of it as follows. Suppose, for a given set of prices of all goods and services, that the welfare, satisfaction or utility of each consumer is a specific and well defined function of his income, that the utility function is the same for all consumers, and that the function is such that each extra dollar of income yields a progressively smaller increment of utility. Utilitarianism is the doctrine that society should seek to maximize the sum of the utilities of all citizens. A legislature might conceivably agree on a utility function and instruct the planner to manage the economy to maximize total utility. Such an instruction would give more or less weight to equality as against total national income according to the curvature of the utility function assigned – the more the function bends, the greater the importance attached to improving the lot of someone whose income is significantly less than the average, and the greater the emphasis on equality would be.

The analogy between planning in a socialist economy and setting the progressivity of the income tax in a capitalist economy is instructive both for the similarities and for the differences. One might, for instance, be inclined to reject planning as contrary to any principle of equity on the grounds that the legislature could never agree on a balance between total income and equality. We must remember, however, that precisely the same problem can and does arise in a capitalist economy in setting rates for old age pensions, unemployment insurance, disability payments and, above all, the progressivity of the income tax. Perhaps a legislature that can set these rates without breaking up into irreconcilable factions can set rules for the planner as well. Vague rules of thumb as to the relative importance of total income and equality may be sufficient.

The analogy is incomplete because the planner has to deal with a range of issues that the tax-setter may avoid. The reason why faction can be avoided in the setting the rate of progressivity in the income tax is that the issue is single-peaked; tax-setting is within the competence of the legislature because the will of the median voter prevails. The planner, on the other hand, has to set prices and wages, assign senior positions in the economy, and make a great variety of decisions that affect the ordering of people in the scale of rich and poor. Only if these decisions can be strictly and rigidly subsumed under a single higher criterion, such as utilitarianism, can the problems of tax-setting and planning be commensurate. We shall see that this cannot be done. The planner will inevitably be called upon to choose among people or groups of people, and the problem of faction described in Chapter 2 will prove insurmountable if one tries to administer socialism on democratic lines.

The setting of prices in a socialist economy has been the subject of a major debate that began in the 1920s, reached its peak in the following decade and continues to crop up from time to time.[4] Known as the 'millions-of-equations' debate, it has to do with whether a planning commission would be able to formulate and solve the enormous system of simultaneous equations, representing the tastes of the different classes of consumers and the available technologies of production, that the competitive economy solves implicitly in establishing prices of all goods and services. It was believed by the opponents of socialism that the setting of prices by a planning commission is so difficult a task, and the prices likely to be arrived at by any conceivable mechanism would be so far from what would really be appropriate, that a socialist economy would prove grossly inefficient; the total national income would fall to a level well below what it would be under capitalism and what a democratic society would accept. Supporters of socialism asserted, on the contrary, that a planning commission under socialism would grope for prices more or less as large efficient firms do in a capitalist economy. Consumer prices would be set to clear the market; excess supply or queues would develop if prices were not quite right; and these in turn would serve as signals as to how prices should be changed. Wages might be set to induce workers to assign themselves appropriately among the available jobs, or workers could be assigned to jobs by the planning commission. Prices of intermediate products could be derived from prices of final goods and services or, as often happens, carried over from capitalist economies where a market does exist. The evidence on the efficiency of large-scale planning is somewhat mixed. Experience in the communist countries shows that planning is not altogether impossible in the sense that people need actually starve, but one's impression of Russia and Eastern Europe is that people are less prosperous than they might be under a different organization of the economy.

Our concern here is not with the efficiency of socialism, but with an issue peripheral to the millions-of-equations debate. Our concern is with the question of whether and to what extent the national income can be assigned to citizens in accordance with a set of general and impersonal rules that the legislature supplies. The accuracy of pricing is important, none the less; for if the planner makes errors or has to exercise a great deal of discretion in the choice of prices, he will be unable to construct accurate measures of efficiency and equality, and will necessarily find himself influencing the assignment of incomes to people because each man's income depends critically on whether particular prices are high or low. A high price of steel would typically, though not necessarily, be accompanied by high wages of steel workers; freight rates affect standards of living in different parts of the country; skill differentials in wage rates necessarily affect the incomes of skilled and unskilled workers. Discretion in price-setting, or less than complete certainty as to the appropriate procedure for choosing prices, weakens the force of the general criteria for the guidance of the economy and paves the way for the introduction of purely political considerations in the assignment of incomes.

But even if efficiency and equality could be measured with tolerable accuracy and a trade-off effected between them, the planner would still be unable to direct the entire economy in accordance with these criteria because of ties among the different alternatives. The following example may serve as a paradigm case. The planner following, let us say, a utilitarian criterion, has to assign three people, Mr A, Mr B and Mr C, to three ranks in a hierarchy, the first with a salary of $30,000, the second with a salary of $20,000 and the third with a salary of $10,000. There is, in practice, no way to distinguish among the qualities of the candidates, and the 'obvious' solution of equalizing their incomes is foreclosed because of its impact elsewhere in the economy. What is the planner to do? Utilitarianism gives no guidance because the sum of the utilities of A, B and C is the same regardless of how the positions are assigned. One might suppose that the planner could flip a coin to break the tie, for if total utility is the same regardless of how the positions are assigned, the choice among the alternatives makes little difference to anyone other than A, B and C, and fairness among them could be established in that way. A random procedure might be satisfactory if utilitarianism could be applied exactly, as it were, to the tenth decimal place. It is unlikely that randomization would prove satisfactory in practice because the utilitarian criterion can never be applied with full precision; and, as anyone who has sat in on a tenure decision knows only too well, there is often as much room for differences of opinion and for unfairness between candidates in deciding that they are equal as in deciding that they are not.

With normal human fallibility and the intrinsic uncertainty in economic affairs, one would expect ties among alternatives to crop up at every turn. Should the new plant be put in this city or that? The national income and the overall distribution of income are not affected to any perceivable extent, but it makes a great deal of difference to the inhabitants of the cities. Should the wage of some class of workers be raised as a means of drawing more skilled people into their line of work? There may be a wide region of indeterminacy because the planner does not know precisely how the quality of workers will be affected by a given change in the wage or what the effect on the final product will be; but the wage makes a great deal of difference to the workers themselves. Should the director of a factory or collective be a Protestant expected to fill subordinate posts with other Protestants or a Jew expected to fill subordinate posts with other Jews? Ties among alternatives are especially likely to arise in procedures for the appointment and removal of people to the senior positions in the economy – the president of a company, the leader of a collective farm, and so on.

One can perhaps imagine what democratic socialism would be like if one thinks of the trouble that democratic countries tend to have in choosing the site of an airport. The significant characteristic of airports from our point of view is that there is no well established principle – no system of equity – for deciding where they ought to be located. The typical situation is that in which most people agree that a new airport is needed, but each man hopes to avoid the noise congestion of the airport by having it located in a part of town away from where he happens to live; and there is no generally accepted criterion for locating the airport in one place or another. Many sites are, of course, ruled out for technical reasons, and the politics begin when the options have been narrowed down to a few sites that are more or less equally satisfactory on criteria such as proximity to centres of population, suitability of the terrain and so on. The different interest groups muster support, and the conflict among them is always unpleasant, often protracted and occasionally violent. It is interesting that such conflicts rarely occur over the location of other types of investment, and then only if the public sector is involved in the decision. The difference is that we have a rule in one case but not in the other. The owner of a firm may establish a new plant where he pleases as long as he acquires the land and does not violate law. There is no comparable procedure for the location of airports, which is another way of saying that our system of equity typically fails to cover that case. Under democratic socialism, the difficulties we encounter in locating new airports, and have learned to cope with when they arise in a limited and carefully circumscribed range of public sector activity, would be encountered in every decision to hire and fire, every choice of what to produce, and every investment in the economy, until the wastage of resources in confrontation and bargaining becomes intolerable, and either socialism or democracy is replaced.

Put more generally, the point we are making is that neither utilitarianism, nor the maximin principle, nor any other rule for balancing total income and equality, is a complete system of equity. Utilitarianism, for instance, fails to apportion the national income among citizens because there are ties, because it is often unclear when alternatives are tied and when they are not, and because, confronted with the possibility of a tie, the planner has no choice but to apply a criterion over and above utilitarianism – in effect, his own best judgement of what is fair and proper in the circumstances – to break the tie.

It might be supposed that these difficulties in choosing among investment projects, while genuine enough, cannot constitute a barrier to democratic socialism – or are no more of a barrier to democracy in a socialist economy than they would be in a capitalist economy — because the identical difficulties arise in choosing investment projects in a large corporation. If these difficulties are insurmountable in the one context, they must surely be so in the other. Even if true, the objection is not decisive, for we cannot rule out the possibility that neither socialism nor capitalism with large corporations is compatible with democracy. What we can do is to point out certain respects in which these difficulties are likely to be more serious in a socialist society than in a capitalist society, even when the latter contains a number of very large corporations. The major difference lies in a quality of the corporation that is often thought of as a source of inferiority to socialist planning as a means of organizing the economy to produce what society requires. While a socialist planning commission under the scrutiny of a democratically elected legislature would, in all probability, be inclined to consider the full ramifications upon society of its investment policy, the director of a privately owned firm need not look beyond the interests of the stockholders in making as much money for the firm as he can. By narrowing the focus of concern, there is provided a rule for directing investment among competing projects, a rule deaf to the diverse claims that would seize the attention of the legislature if the legislature were to exert an influence on the course of events.

The difference between socialism and capitalism in this respect depends, of course, on the structure of industry. At one extreme, where the whole economy is organized as one large firm with all citizens as shareholders, the problems we have been attributing to socialism would reappear as conflict among groups of stockholders competing for advantages to their trades, localities or social classes. The problems diminish as the number of firms increase and as the special and individual interests of stockholders become progressively subordinate to their common interest in the profitability of the firm. At the other extreme, in a fully competitive economy with a great many small firms, the composition of investment in the economy as a whole could be determined in complete independence of the legislature, though the legislature might, if it wished, take a hand in the matter through taxation or tariff policy, reintroducing some of the problems of political assignment. We shall return to the question of monopoly when we consider capitalist equity in the next chapter. What is essential at this point is that no general rule the legislature might impose upon the planner is sufficient to bind the planner in every particular of his direction of the economy. The legislature in a socialist society must either trust the planner with enormous discretionary power over the lives and careers of citizens, or take a major role in the direction of the economy, accepting the massive political assignment of income and other advantages that the role would imply.

A socialist equity may none the less be possible if the planner is seen as one whose judgement, sense of fairness and perspicacity are so reliable that the legislature can desist from involving itself in the management of the economy once the initial criteria are supplied. It is doubtful whether this would be so. The legislature might be content to supply the planning commission with a general criterion, and otherwise to desist from intervening in the economy, if the planning commission could be counted on to translate the general criterion into a complete set of rules for the management of the economy and the assignment of income and status among citizens. I believe it beyond the capacity of pressure groups in a democratic society to exercise such restraint when everyone knows that the general criterion is insufficient.

The difficulty is compounded when we turn from the task of the planner in organizing the economy to the task of the legislature in choosing the planner. The legislature might limit itself to the appointment of a head planner given tenure for a substantial period of time and allowed to appoint the rest of the planning commission, which would in turn supervise the industrial hierarchy, set wages and establish targets or other rules for the individual enterprises to follow. Alternatively, the legislature might concern itself with the appointment of all major posts in the planning and industrial hierarchy, more or less as the president and legislature in the United States determine the occupancy of the major posts in the US government, and there might be quite detailed instructions as to how the economy is to be conducted. Regardless of which procedure is adopted, the legislature cannot avoid choosing policy in its choice of personnel, and it cannot be unaware of the effects of its choice upon the assignment of income. One candidate for the directorship of the planning commission supports high farm prices and is inclined to favour people from the Mid West. Another candidate favours free trade in farm products and picks his appointments from a different stratum of society. Factions develop over the choice among candidates. Candidates for the head of the planning commission, anxious to get the job, slant their policies towards perceived interests in the legislature. Each geographic, racial, linguistic or ethnic group and each political party acquires an incentive to seek assurances from a prospective planner that its interests will not be overlooked.

It is, in any case, beyond the capacity of a democratic society to prevent the different economic and social classes from using political power to further their ends. Farmers, trade unions, big business, environmentalists and ethnic associations all have their pressure groups to which politicians must give some weight if they wish to remain in office. At present in Europe and America, the power of pressure groups to influence the assignment of income is limited by the existence of a private sector where the greater part of most people's income is still determined. Take away the private sector and transfer the means of production to the state, and the conflict among pressure groups intensifies enormously, because it is in the legislature, and in the legislature alone, that one's income and status in society are established.

The characteristics of our 15-man example begin to emerge in the conflict over the direction of the planned economy. Each interest group is constantly in fear that a coalition may form behind its back to support a planner who will, in turn, use his authority in the interests of his supporters. Fear leads to the formation of coalitions that might not otherwise be established. Each candidate for the post of planner is compelled to say in great detail how he would manage the economy and who would be favoured under his regime. An atmosphere develops in which strength is to be found in association with likeminded people. Group loyalties and antagonism among groups intensify, leading first to an escalation of political activity as it becomes progressively more important who sits in the legislature and on the planning commission, then to economic warfare as each social group seeks to impress upon the legislature how nasty it can be if its interests are ignored, and finally to outright violence as a last resort.

The struggle is intensified still further by the power of the bureaucracy under socialism and the absence of alternative employment for those removed from senior posts in a change of government. Where there is a large private sector, it can serve as a refuge for bureaucrats and politicians out of office and as a nurturing ground for the opposition. Socialism, as defined here, removes the private sector, making it particularly difficult for the opposition to form and for anyone removed from office to find his feet again. The ruling party can use its authority over the economy to block the opposition at every turn. The opposition can be denied access to the press and other media of communication. Potential opposition supporters can be intimidated by threats to their jobs and to their prospects for advancement. The news can be manipulated to show the ruling party to advantage. When all else fails, the ruling party can use its authority over the army and the police to render the opposition ineffectual or to abolish democratic government altogether. In such an environment, a fall from office through an adverse vote in the legislature is a fall from the very top to the very bottom of society, for the ex-members of Parliament have no choice but to accept positions in hierarchies directly under the control of their successors. Sooner or later, a society where the economy is run on socialist principles would come under the control of the administration class which, being organized as a hierarchy, must necessarily place supreme authority in a king, an emperor or a chairman of the only legitimate political party.

5

Capitalism as a System of Equity

All ownership derives from occupation and violence. When we consider the natural components of goods, apart from the labour components they contain, and when we follow the legal title back, we must necessarily arrive at a point where this title originated in the appropriation of goods available to all. Before that, we may encounter a forcible expropriation from a predecessor whose ownership we can, in turn, trace to an earlier appropriation or robbery. That all rights derive from violence, all ownership from appropriation or robbery, we may freely admit . . .

Ludwig von Mises[1]

Does capitalism, as we know it, contain a system of equity? This is not an easy question to answer, for what goes by the name of capitalism is, in reality, an immensely complex form of organization with elements of private ownership, to be sure, but with socialistic elements in the organization of basic research, public ownership of some industries and regulation of others, with a substantial not-for-profit sector which has no place in either socialist or capitalist models, and with varying degrees of monopoly. The very existence of government rules out a perfect and complete system of equity. The question becomes whether capitalism, as it has evolved, allows a large enough share of the national income to be assigned independently of the political arena for democracy to continue.

The proof of the existence of competitive equilibrium is relevant but not decisive. It is relevant because it identifies the source of equity in a capitalist economy and because it suggests how equity might be reinforced through the judicious choice of economic policy. The theory of general equilibrium tells us that in an economy where all resources are privately owned, where producers utilize their resources to make as much money as they can, where consumers spend their income to maximize their welfare and where contracts, as it were, enforce themselves — in such an economy, there emerges a unique set of prices at which markets for all goods and services are cleared (everything for sale has a buyer and there is no unfilled demand); and that these prices, in turn, supply us with a unique and totally non-political assignment of incomes among people in the economy. The absence of the government from the model, though unrealistic, does at least show that assignment can be attended to in the private sector alone. In sharp contrast to socialism, the perfectly competitive economy yields an assignment that is feasible as a system of equity in the sense that the acceptance of the rules would henceforth remove assignment from the political arena altogether.

The proof of the existence of general equilibrium is not decisive as an argument for the proposition that actual capitalism contains a system of equity, because actual capitalism differs greatly from the model and because the assignment of incomes in a perfectly competitive economy need not be acceptable. There may well be a trade-off between acceptability and feasibility. If, as is often asserted but never to my knowledge proved or disproved, perfect competition would be unacceptable because of its distributional consequences, then a degree of political intervention may be required to equalize the distribution of income, even at the cost of making the system of equity less feasible than it might otherwise be.

It is tempting to try to take an empirical shortcut in this analysis. One might suppose that the way to tell what sort of economic arrangements can coexist with democracy is to study the historical and contemporary evidence. One need not be a full-fledged economic determinist to suppose that the kinds of economies observed in countries deemed to be more or less democratic are the kinds of economies compatible with democratic government, and that forms of economic organization not so far seen to coexist with democratic government have probably failed to do so because they are technically incompatible. The presumption is that an economy like that in the United States creates pressure towards a government like that in the United States, and an economy like that in the Soviet Union creates pressure towards a government like that in the Soviet Union. Without denying the relevance or importance of historical evidence on this matter, I would insist that it cannot serve as a substitute for an analysis of the logic of the connection between economic and political arrangements.

There is, first, a problem of timing. Political institutions change slowly, and democracy may persist for quite some time in a country after the economic prerequisite has gone. Pure empiricism could lead us astray. Pure empiricism could lead us to imagine that a certain mix of economic arrangements is favourable to democracy when, in fact, the democracy we observe is the product of quite a different economy and is currently being undermined. Of greater importance is the fact that empiricism does not tell us which features of an economy are conducive to democracy. This would not matter if our only choice were between an economic organization exactly like that in the Soviet Union and an economic organization exactly like that in the United States. But societies seldom, if ever, get to make choices of that kind. Economic institutions have momentum, changes come gradually, and observation alone will not tell us whether a particular change is favourable to democracy. Consider the question of whether democracy would, on balance, be strengthened or weakened by allowing firemen the right to strike. I do not wish to get into the substance of the question, but suppose, for the sake of the argument, that allowing firemen to strike would be favourable to democracy. This could not be inferred from observations of what democracies do because the evidence is mixed – some democracies allow firemen to strike while others do not – because what is best for democracy in one time and place may not be so in another, and because not all aspects of economic policy in democratic countries need be conducive to democracy. Policies may be adopted for reasons other than the preservation of democracy. It could well happen that all democratic countries prohibit firemen from striking even though democratic government would work marginally better otherwise. The slight harm done by the anti-strike policy might be substantially overbalanced by pro-democratic policies elsewhere in the economy. Finally, and most important, observation untainted by theorizing gives little guidance when it comes to reform. There is no assurance that economic institutions that have coexisted with democracy in the past can continue to do so. Technical innovation, social change or economic growth itself, if unaccompanied by new institutions, could enhance the role of the legislature in the assignment of incomes or could give rise to an unacceptably large spread between the incomes of the rich and the poor.

Our analysis of capitalist equity is developed around two main questions: (1) does capitalism, as we know it and as it seems to be evolving, contain enough of a system of equity for democracy to continue? and (2) what are the probable effects upon the system of equity of the different kinds of economic policy a democratic society may adopt? We take up the first of these questions in the present chapter and the second in the next and final chapter in the book. This chapter is divided into four sections; the first three are about how monopoly, government and the incomplete tenure of property may affect the feasibility of capitalism, and the fourth is an analysis of why capitalism might be acceptable to the majority of voters.

MONOPOLY

It is arguable that capitalism – capitalism as it is, and not as portrayed in our models – contains no system of equity at all. The model, so the argument goes, portrays the interaction of many tiny firms in a competitive market; the reality is a mixture of rivalry and accommodation among giant firms, and the tendency of capitalism is for firms to get bigger and bigger until there is just one huge firm in each industry. The government, which may at that point be a committee of directors of the major firms, would have no alternative but to set prices as a means of avoiding the chaos from commercial rivalry among gigantic monopolists. By setting prices, the government necessarily determines the profits in the different firms and the incomes of their owners. Though it is conceivable for competition among workers to equalize wages, it seems more likely that workers, in these circumstances, would be organized in one or more great unions and that wages as well as prices would have to be determined as part of an overall political settlement. The rivalry among firms in pursuit of sales and among workers in pursuit of jobs, the intra-class rivalry that is the driving force of competition, would be eliminated, and society would find itself in a position not fundamentally different from our 15-man example where voters cannot avoid having to apportion the national income among themselves.

There are really two sides to this argument. There is the factual question of whether capitalism is moving towards a world of monopolies, and there is the theoretical question of whether a world of monopolies, if it comes to that, contains a system of equity. As to the theoretical question, I think the argument is correct. A world of monopolies contains no system of equity that I can discern and would require that income be assigned politically.[2]

This may be seen in a simple example[3] often used in the classroom exposition of the theory of general equilibrium. Suppose there are just two goods, bread produced by farmers and cheese produced by cattlemen. If there are a great many independent farmers and a great many independent cattlemen, then a unique price (a unique rate of exchange between bread and cheese) will emerge as farmers and cattlemen come together in the market to buy and sell. The price plays a dual role of clearing the market for bread and cheese and of apportioning the total income between farmers and cattlemen. That there exists such a price should be obvious from one's experience of markets, especially country markets, where the conditions of this example come close to being fulfilled. Its existence is proved formally in the theory of general equilibrium. A farmer who demands a higher price will find no buyers, and a farmer who foolishly offers bread at a lower price will be asked to sell more than he can supply. The market will not work unless the state enforces contracts and property rights, but that is all the state needs to do. It is the essence of capitalist equity that the state need take no direct role in establishing or influencing the price itself.

To see how monopoly affects capitalist equity, let us now suppose that all of the available land is divided up into two great collective farms, one containing all the farm land suitable for production of bread and the other containing all the grazing land suitable for the production of cheese. To ensure that trade actually takes place, and to rule out the possibility of each collective farm becoming self-sufficient, let us also suppose that no cheese can be produced on farm land, that no bread can be produced on grazing land, and that both bread and cheese are required in the diet. As before, the incomes of farmers and cattlemen depend critically upon the relative price of bread and cheese, but the price is no longer established automatically through buying and selling in the market. Farmers naturally want a high price for bread and can now insist upon it because, in the absence of competition among farmers, no individual farmer can take advantage of a situation where other farmers withhold bread from the market. Cattlemen also act in concert. They can demand a low price for bread and refuse to sell cheese at all unless they get it. Thus, farmers are offering to sell bread at, say, two loaves per pound of cheese while cattlemen are willing to buy bread only at four loaves per pound of cheese, and there is no mechanism within the market to bring these prices together because it is precisely the mechanism for doing so that is eliminated when production of bread and cheese is monopolized.

To be sure, a trade of bread for cheese will eventually take place, but as the market can no longer find a price, society must come to rely on direct negotiation between the two producer collectives. It is a negotiation without clear principles as to how total income is to be divided between farmers and cattlemen, where both parties hold in reserve the threat to cease trading altogether, and where the mutual threat to cease trading, coupled with the requirement that some trade must ultimately take place, may give rise to violence at any time. Let there be 15 industries instead of just two, and we have reproduced the essential features of our example in Chapter 2 of an economy with no system of equity whatsoever. Thus far, the argument that monopoly destroys capitalistic equity is valid: if the natural tendency of capitalist development is towards monopoly, and if this tendency cannot be contained well short of the limit discussed here, then what we are calling capitalist equity will, in time, be attenuated and the economic prerequisite of democracy will be lost.

To grant this proposition — and I fail to see how it can be denied — immediately raises two issues that are difficult to resolve but of great importance for our assessment of the degree of compatibility of capitalism and democracy. The first is whether there is a feasible system of equity associated with industrial structures neither perfectly competitive nor perfectly monopolized, but in between. In other words, how far from the competitive ideal can the economy go, and how closely can it approach pure monopoly before the system of equity is destroyed? The other issue has to do with trends: are there forces in society conducive to monopoly, can such tendencies to monopoly as may exist be contained, and what light can be shed on this issue by the history of industrial structure in capitalist countries?

Our assessment of the degree of equity in economies where the industrial organization is neither perfectly competitive nor completely monopolized cannot be other than impressionistic, for the economics of the middle ground which goes by the names of oligopoly, imperfect competition or monopolistic competition gives no clear guidance as to how firms behave. However, there is at least one case that is easily analysed. The indeterminacy in price formation we observed when two monopolists confront one another is eliminated when a single monopolist confronts an otherwise competitive economy. If the farmers were monopolized but the cattlemen were not, then the farmers would set a price that the cattlemen would take as given, and the indeterminacy we have been discussing, with the corresponding need for political assignment through price-setting, would not arise. Similarly, political assignment could be avoided in an economy with several monopolies in industries small enough and sufficiently independent of one another that each monopolist is inclined to set his price regardless of the prices of the others. An economy where the only monopolies are to be found in peanuts, lettuce and teacups would work like an economy with a single monopoly. But as already shown in the bread and cheese example, we cannot generalize from the case where there is one monopoly or a few unrelated monopolies to the case where large portions of the economy are monopolized and the different monopolies recognize their interdependence.

Two distinctions are important for our assessment of the effect of monopoly on the capitalist system of equity. The first is the distinction between monopoly and monopolization. A monopoly may be inefficient in the sense that the national income would be greater if the industry were competitive, but the existence of the monopoly need not imply that anyone is getting an abnormally high return on his investment. Suppose that for hundreds of years the right to sell cheese has been the exclusive property of the Royal Cheese Monopoly. If the monopoly has any permanence at all, the value of the shares in the cheese company must exceed the value of the assets of the company. That does not imply that shareholders are earning an abnormal return on their investment, because the present shareholders purchased their shares at a price reflecting the present value of the monopoly profit, while the original beneficiaries of the patent of monopoly are long since dead, their mono-poly profits consumed in their lifetimes or passed on to heirs, most of whom no longer hold shares in the cheese monopoly. There is a saying in public finance that an old tax is a good tax. For precisely the same reason, an old monopoly is a good monopoly; its beneficiaries are untraceable, the present owners of the monopoly are not on a different footing from owners of any other kind of property, and capitalist equity is not impaired.

Monopolization is entirely different. Unlike normal trade, it is a way of making money at the expense of the rest of society. If a firm in com-petition invests in a factory and if the investment is profitable, the value of what is produced in the factory must exceed the cost of the resources used to produce it. The appearance of the new factory affects prices to some extent, making some people worse off and others better off, but on balance the gains cannot be less than the losses, and the rest of the population (everyone other than the owners of the firm) cannot be worse off in the aggregate than they were before. If an industry is monopolized, the gain to the owners of the firms that make up the monopoly is outweighed by a corresponding loss to the rest of the pop-ulation. Monopolization restricts output to raise price; the monopolist gains from the higher price, while the rest of the population must nec-essarily lose both from the rise in price and from the corresponding reduction in output. In fact, the gain to the monopolist is somewhat less than the loss to the rest of society because both parties lose from the reduction in output. It is for this reason that a society that might tolerate well established monopolies has a marked interest in preventing formation of new ones. The case against monopolization, as opposed to mere monopoly, is very like the case against theft. An individual or group wants to take something from the rest of the population, and it is in the interest of the rest of the population to prevent him from doing so.

It is, I believe, as a consequence of the anti-social nature of monopoli-zation that monopoly, where it does exist, is generally incomplete and imperfect from the monopolists' point of view. There is an uneasy balance between the monopolist who would like to raise prices more than he does and the government that one way or another is prepared to discipline the monopolist if prices are raised beyond certain limits.[4] The medical association may succeed in raising doctors' fees somewhat through the control of entry to medical schools, but medical schools are obliged to train more doctors than the medical profession would choose if unconstrained by pressure from government and public opinion. The American automobile companies may exercise some monopoly power (it is uncertain whether the three major companies should be thought of as competition or monopoly), but the extent of that power is surely limited by the government's control of the height of the tariff on foreign cars. The seamen's union exercises some monopoly power in its control of entry, but the extent of that power is limited by the government's control of the subsidy to domestic shipping. Natural monopolies, such as railroads and telephones, are usually regulated, though it is often claimed that the regulators become, in time, the agents of the regulated. And, of course, anti-trust is empowered to prohibit a variety of business practices believed to be conducive to monopoly, or to break up monopoly where it is found to exist.

The second distinction is between monopolies and large firms. Typically, monopolies are either large firms, like US Steel or Standard Oil before they were broken up, or large collections of firms organized in a cartel. But not all large firms are monopolies. Actual competition from other firms, large or small, and potential competition from firms that could enter the market if the large firm chooses to raise prices may constitute an effective check on the power of the large firm to do so. Conglomerate firms in many businesses at once would seem to compete vigorously with one another, each ready to enter a new line of business whenever profits seem above normal or innovations present the opportunity to cut into the sales in an established line of products.

It is debatable whether bigness itself should be a matter of public concern. Some authors feel that it should not unless there is evidence of monopoly pricing or the intent to monopolize. Others argue that a trend towards ever larger firms must, in the end, lead to the monopolization of large segments of industry and will, in any case, tend to foster an alliance between big business and government in which large firms reap special advantages not available to others. Large firms may not be allowed to fail because the dislocation of labour and capital would be considered excessive. British Leyland and Lockheed were kept going by the governments of their respective countries though many small firms equal in total employment were allowed to go bankrupt.[5] A large firm may use its leverage as the dominant employer in a city or state to enlist the local politician to support its interests in procuring government contracts or in the imposition of tariffs or quotas on the import of competing products.

Returning to our main theme, we can say that a form of industrial organization which is neither perfectly competitive nor fully monopolized, where there is some monopoly and many large firms, must involve the government in the assignment of income at several critical points. The government may have to break a deadlock in wage bargaining where a union representing all workers in an industry confronts an association of all firms in the industry and where the wage is no more determined by market forces than is the price in our bread and cheese example. The government may intervene because a prolonged strike is considered harmful to the nation, but it cannot intervene without, at the same time, influencing the wage that is ultimately set. In fact, recognition by union and management that the government will ultimately intervene may create intransigence on both sides in the initial negotiation.[6] The government cannot avoid having to influence the assignment of income in regulating the professions and in setting the rules for natural monopolies like telephones and railways where there is a constant tension between the regulated firm wishing to raise prices and the rest of society hoping prices can be held down. And, whether it ought to or not, the government tends to get drawn into matters involving the interests of any firm large enough to enlist the support of the elected representatives in its locality. The extent to which incomes are assigned in the legislature rather than by the market increases with the amount of monopoly in the economy. Perfect competition has a perfectly feasible system of equity. A world of monopolies, as exemplified by the bread and cheese example, contains no system of equity. Somewhere between perfect competition and pure monopoly is a line beyond which the system of equity is not sufficient for democratic government to continue. I think it unlikely that the line has already been crossed in Canada or the United States, though I would find it difficult to justify that assertion.

But the case against capitalism as a system of equity rests not so much on an assessment of industrial organization today as on a perception of trends. The argument is that unalterable trends in technology and industrial organizations must eventually lead to a crossing of the line beyond which the economy is too monopolized for democratic government to continue. One can think of several reasons why this might be so. Technical change may be making the development of new and better products increasingly dependent on large-scale industrial research, which is more easily amortized in large firms than in small ones and which is more likely to pay off if the firm has many lines of output to which the intrinsically unpredictable discoveries of its research lab may be applied. Economies of scale from research can be expected to become progressively greater as scientific equipment becomes more sophisticated and expensive and as team work comes more and more to replace individual endeavour.

The increasing sophistication of the products themselves may create a situation where the optimal scale of a firm approaches the size of the market for its products. This would seem to be particularly likely in defence industries where a single product, a new aeroplane or missile, can cost tens of billions of dollars and is beyond the capacity of all but a few giant firms to supply. Or contrast the industrial organization of offshore exploration for oil with the industrial organization of gold prospecting in the nineteenth century. The former involves projects that only consortia of giant firms are large enough to undertake and where profitability depends critically on a continuing negotiation with host governments, while the latter consisted for the most part, of prospectors working entirely alone.

Optimal scale is also increased by the precautions that must be undertaken to ensure product safety and quality control. Science is developing more and more potentially lethal substances, and the ordinary man has ever less capacity to judge which products are safe and which are not. How can I know whether a given hairdye is likely to cause me to have cancer in 20 years' time, whether a particular fertilizer or ingredient in cattle feed is likely to be dangerous, or whether a cure for morning sickness will result in defective children? A firm that wishes to put a new product onto the market must be obliged to undertake an extensive and costly programme of testing, and the government must ultimately decide when a product is safe and when it is not. One cannot depend on the right of the injured party to sue for damages because a small firm can often escape payment through bankruptcy and because the potential harmfulness of a product may be to the environment and not just to the user, in which case injury cannot normally be traced to its source. Be that as it may, the legal requirement for the extensive testing of new substances is a barrier to entry of new firms and, as products become ever more difficult to analyse, a source of increasing returns to scale in industries where new types of products are important. The establishment of facilities to test new products may be more costly than the establishment of facilities to produce them, especially for a new firm that wishes to begin with a narrow product line.

Large firms may be acquiring an edge over their smaller rivals through the development of new products and processes that reduce the cost of transport, communication and accounting. Television has proved beneficial to firms with sales large enough to justify the high cost of advertising in that medium. At least one major disadvantage of large firms with many plants throughout the country, namely the difficulty of controlling the activities of the different plants from a single headquarters, has been largely neutralized over the last thirty years by computers, more efficient telephone service and cheap air fares. It is unlikely that the replacement of independent restaurants, groceries, clothing stores and so on by large, nationwide chains would have been possible but for changes in the means of communication among the branches.[7]

There is reason for concern that the natural tendency of technical change may be to foster an industrial organization with progressively fewer and larger firms and with diminished competition among them. Yet there is nothing inevitable about such a development. Nothing in the preceding argument ensures that firms will grow without limit or rules out the possibility that technical change may be yielding a series of new products best made by relatively small firms. Large organizations, with many layers of hierarchy, may lack the flexibility for innovation, and firms may actually become smaller on average as innovation becomes increasingly important. There are enough examples of innovation in large firms and of innovation in small firms to rule out the simple propositions that only in large firms or only in small ones can innovation occur.

A tendency towards ever larger firms owing to increasing economies of scale — if such a tendency exists at all — may be opposed through public policy. Monopolies and very large firms may be required to subdivide, or an incentive to subdivide may be provided by making the corporation tax progressive, so that two small firms would pay less tax than one large firm if their total size — measured by assets, sales or profits — were the same. Though there is a presumption that the most efficient size of firm is increasing in most industries, there is no iron law and there is no reason to suppose that a trend towards ever larger firms cannot be halted or reversed.

With these considerations in mind, we might look briefly at the evidence of the history of the competitiveness of capitalist economies. The trend towards competition or monopoly can be assessed from data on the size of firms or from data on the degree of concentration in industries. An example of the first type of measure is the share of total manufacturing output accounted for by the 100 largest firms. Using this measure one would say that a country is becoming more monopolized if the share of the 100 largest firms is growing over time. An example of the other measure is the share of a particular industry or class of products accounted for by the four largest firms in the industry or product line. The economy may be said to be becoming more monopolistic if the average of the four-firm concentration ratios is increasing over time.

For the United Kingdom and the United States, the evidence on the share in total net manufacturing output of the 100 largest enterprises is shown in figure 5.1. The share has increased in both countries over the whole of the period from 1910 to 1972, but the rate of growth, which accelerated in the United Kingdom since the Second World War, has levelled off in the United States, suggesting that the British economy is becoming increasingly monopolized while the American economy is not. The evidence on concentration ratios is more difficult to summarize and to assess, and I will not attempt to do so except to cite what I take to be the opinion of the most informed students of industrial organization:

Figure 5.1. Shares of 100 largest enterprises in manufacturing net output, United Kingdom and United States

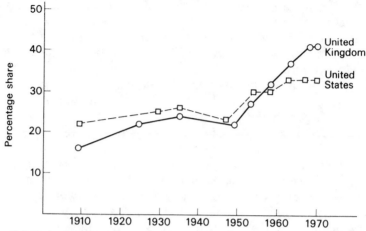

Source: S.J. Prais, *The Evolution of Giant Firms in Britain,* Cambridge University Press, 1976, page 140

that concentration in the United States has neither increased nor decreased to any significant extent since the turn of the century.[8] These apparently contradictory pieces of evidence may perhaps be reconciled if we suppose that, on balance, firms have become larger but more diverse so that product-by-product competition is not less than it used to be.

Why the trends are what they are is difficult to say. It may be that technical change has not, on balance, been especially favourable to the growth of big firms, or it may be that the anti-trust laws have been successful in controlling a natural tendency towards monopoly. Whatever the reason, there appears to be no significant slide into monopoly in the United States and the threat from that quarter to the capitalist system of equity does not, at the moment, appear to have materialized.

GOVERNMENT

The public sector is necessarily a socialist enclave in an otherwise capitalist economy. This is not a statement about political attitudes of civil servants or politicians, whose views would presumably extend over the whole range from extreme socialism to extreme capitalism. It is an assertion that the assignment of incomes and other advantages in the public sector is in accordance with principles quite different from those in the private sector and more or less in accord with the principles by which the whole of national income would have to be assigned in a socialist state. Capitalist equity assigns incomes to citizens in accordance with the earnings of the human and non-human factors in production they possess. Other principles are required for drawing the line between public and private sectors, deciding on the size of the budget, allocating total expenditure among the different items in the budget, determining how and from whom the tax revenue will be raised, and in recruiting and promoting civil servants. We argued at length in Chapter 4 that there is no system of equity, no feasible and acceptable method of assigning incomes independently of the political arena, in a society where the economy is run on socialist lines. The question now becomes whether a partially socialist economy is any better — whether the pitfalls of democracy in an entirely socialist economy can be avoided in a partly socialist economy called capitalism. Is there, in other words, a system of public sector equity for a capitalist economy? Is there a way of assigning the benefits and burdens of government activity in accordance with rules sufficiently well-established and sufficiently acceptable to the majority of voters that the conflicts among voters that destroy democracy in our 15-man example in Chapter 2 can be kept at bay?

The question becomes increasingly important with the growth of the public sector. Over the last half century the share of government expenditure inclusive of transfer payments has increased from 16 to 42 per cent in Canada, from 10 to 33 per cent in the United States and from 24 to 50 per cent in the United Kingdom. As Table 5.1 shows, the growth has been erratic, with huge increases to finance the Second World War, sharp declines immediately thereafter, and a gradual rise throughout the 1960s and early 1970s, with a levelling off in the last few years. But the initial and terminal years of the table, years without war or deep depression, are comparable as markers for the long-term trend. Approximately half of the growth of government expenditure is attributable to expenditure on goods and services, and the other half is attributable to transfer payments. The growth of government is like the growth of monopoly, in that either trend, continued long enough, would abolish capitalist equity; but one cannot help feeling that government expenditure is closer than monopoly to the edge of what democracy can tolerate, and — the American tax revolt notwithstanding — there is no real assurance that the trend towards greater public expenditure has come to an end. The immediate question is whether the government is not already too large and powerful for a non-political method of assignment to be maintained.[9] This, in turn, depends on whether capitalist equity can be supplemented by other principles of equity for the public sector.

The curious feature of public sector equity is its diversity. While the assignment of income under pure capitalism rests on the single principle that each man gets the value of the earnings of his factors of production, public sector assignment rests on many partly conflicting and partly complementary principles, each with its own domain of application. In

Table 5.1. The growth of government expenditure in Canada, the United States and the United Kingdom (percentages of gross national product)

	Canada		United States		United Kingdom	
	a Total government expenditure inclusive of transfer payments	b Government expenditure on goods and services	a Total government expenditure inclusive of transfer payments	b Government expenditure on goods and services	a Total government expenditure inclusive of transfer payments	b Government expenditure on goods and services
	%	%	%	%	%	%
1929	16	10	10	9	24	12
1933	27	13	19	15	26	13
1944	50	42	49	46	73	59
1950	22	13	21	14	39	22
1955	27	18	25	19	37	23
1960	30	18	30	20	40	22
1965	30	20	27	20	43	24
1970	36	23	32	22	47	27
1973	37	22	31	21	47	26
1975	41	24	35	22	55	30
1978	42	24	33	21	50	26

Sources: Canada: R.M. Bird, *The Growth of Government Spending in Canada,* Canadian Tax Foundation, 1970, Table 33, updated from 1967 with *The National Finances,* Canadian Tax Foundation, various years;
United States: *The National Income and Product Accounts of the United States 1929–74,* US Department of Commerce, updated from the US national accounts in the July issue of the *Survey of Current Business;*
United Kingdom: A. Peacock and J. Wiseman, *The Growth of Public Expenditure in England,* Princeton University Press, 1961, Tables A5, A2, A12, updated from *National Income and Expenditure,* Central Statistical Office, various years. These data do not include investment of public corporations. For the U.K. only, the gross national product is measured at factor cost. Thus, while the trend is probably right, the numbers have to be reduced by about 5 percentage points to make them comparable with the series for Canada and the U.S.

fact, all of the systems of equity discussed in Chapter 2 have a role to play in the assignment of income and other advantages in the public sector.

Equality has a primary role to play in voting. Every citizen is equal to every other citizen in his direct influence through the ballot box upon the choice of public officials and, if the political process works as it is supposed to do, in his indirect influence through his elected representatives upon the content of policy in foreign and domestic affairs. It would be surprising if this essential equality among people as voters did not conflict at many points with the essential inequality among people as owners of dollars of purchasing power in the market sector of the economy.

Equality extends naturally from voting on public policy to the allocation of services supplied by the public sector. When supplied in the private sector, services are assigned to those who choose to pay for them. When supplied in the public sector, they are frequently, though not always, assigned equally to all citizens. Elementary education is a case in point. Our ideal, if not our practice, is that every child is to have an equal educational opportunity, and that differences in outcome be attributable only to the different capacities of children to respond to a common opportunity. Secondary education is sometimes assigned equally, though the merit principle (to be discussed below) has a large role to play as, for instance, when only particularly bright students are admitted into certain programmes. Medical services are usually assigned equally if, and in so far as, they are supplied by the public sector. In Canada, a minimum pension is assigned to everyone over 65 years of age, and there is an additional sum related to the former earnings of the recipient. Equality may also be important on the revenue side of the budget. It is obviously the principle underlying the poll tax (each person pays the same dollar value of tax), but it has been subtly extended as a justification for the progressive income tax. The progressive income tax has been advocated as a means of making each taxpayer bear the same sacrifice in the payment of the tax (the richer one is, the less of a sacrifice of welfare does he bear in the payment of any given number of dollars of tax) or, more directly, as a means of ensuring that the distribution of income after tax will be more equal than the original distribution of income.

Cost-benefit analysis is a system of equity within its domain of application; it is an impersonal and non-political procedure for assigning benefits and costs of public sector activity. Reduced to simplest terms, the rules of cost-benefit analysis are a set of instructions to the planner to proceed with the given project – the building of a road, bridge, dam or airport, whatever the project may be – if, all things considered, the national income is larger with the project than without it. In this calculation, only dollar values of costs and benefits are recognized and no account is taken of the identity of the beneficiaries. Costs and benefits are weighed on a common scale, 'to whomsoever they may accrue'. Society is prepared to tolerate this deliberate and self-imposed blindness on the part of the planner because a policy of maximizing national income can be expected to benefit most people in the long run because no one knows in advance who the beneficiaries and who the losers will be, and above all, in my opinion, because an objective and impersonal rule – any such rule – is preferable to the confusion that would arise, and does arise, when decisions are based on purely political compromises among legislators. Our airport example in Chapter 4 was of a large project where cost-benefit rules were not strictly applied or political pressures became important in the event of a tie between alternatives. Though the rules are different, cost-benefit analysis plays a role in the assignment of income in the public sector similar to that played by the institution of property in the private sector. Both are efficient in the sense of leading to outcomes from which no further benefits to everyone are possible, and both enable the legislature to keep its distance from the direct assignment of income.

Capitalist equity plays an important role in the public sector. Tickets for rides on the state railway are sold, not distributed equally among citizens. Wages of employees in the public sector are set in accordance with wages of comparable jobs in the private sector because that is considered an equitable course to follow and because public sector wages cannot fall short of private sector wages if suitable workers are to be hired. In general, the public sector is expected to purchase goods and services as inexpensively as possible, exactly as a private firm making the same purchase would be inclined to do. The application of capitalist equity to the public sector requires the public sector to use whatever residual discretion it may have to set prices and wages as they would be if the activities in question had been undertaken in the private sector.

Even *feudal equity* may have a role in public sector assignment. Some authors have claimed that tariffs, subsidies and agricultural price supports are administered according to a 'conservative' principle to counteract the effects on particular groups of producers of sharp declines in world prices or other market forces that would affect their income adversely. Such behaviour on the part of the public sector would be more nearly consistent with what we have called feudal equity than with policy conducive to equality because the parties whose incomes are preserved through tariffs or subsidies could be rich or poor. A policy of protecting incomes from market forces will not, on balance, be equalizing, unless – and there is no reason to suppose this to be so – the beneficiaries are, on the whole, less well off than the average of the population.

The *lottery*, as a system of equity, could be classified as a variant of equality though it does not yield equality of results. Jury duty is frequently assigned by lot. Military service is assigned by lot when there is conscription, but less than the whole of each cohort of young men is required in the army. The lottery has been used extensively in the city states of the ancient world and medieval Europe to assign positions of authority without, at the same time, developing a ruling class that might seek to overthrow democratic government.

The principle of *merit* is used for access to higher education. Places are assigned to students who score the best grades on competitive examinations. The practice might be justified on the utilitarian ground that the benefits of education, to the educated and to the public at large, are greatest when education is provided to those who can prove themselves most capable of learning and applying what they learn; but it is sometimes claimed that selection by merit is appropriate in itself regardless of the consequences. In either case, selection by merit is a procedure with a family resemblance to cost-benefit analysis, yet sufficiently distinctive to warrant treatment as a separate system of public sector equity. The principle of merit is like the principle of equality in one sense but not in another. It is like equality in that candidates for desirable positions are judged independently of their wealth and social position; it is the means by which children from poor families may advance. It is unlike equality in that it tends to reinforce and magnify the advantages of natural talent and of family influence upon the capacity for education of the child. If, and in so far as, educated workers can earn the value of their marginal products, the education of one extra person conveys no benefit to the rest of the population because he can expect to earn the value of his net contribution to society. Subsidization of the education of talented people is anti-egalitarian, in so far as it transfers income to the talented, who would in any case earn higher than average incomes.

An immediate consequence of the multiplicity of the forms of public sector equity is the ever-present possibility that they may conflict. An interesting, though by no means the most important, instance of this conflict arises in the assessment of the costs of fatal accidents. In the building of roads or airports, a decision has frequently had to be made as to whether a given improvement in safety, brought about, for instance, by installing a clover-leaf junction or sophisticated equipment for air traffic control, is worth the cost. Now the standard procedure in evaluating benefits in cost-benefit analysis – the only practical way to compare kilowatts of electricity from a hydro-electric project, time saved from an improvement in road construction and the loss of private consumption from the taxes required to finance such projects on a common scale – is to accept private evaluations in all things. All dollars-worth of benefit are equal, regardless of the identity of the beneficiary. Normally, this means that all units of a given type of output are treated as equivalent benefits, no matter who the recipient may be, because arbitrage can be counted upon to equalize valuations among consumers. A can of beans is worth the same amount of money to a rich man as to a poor man because both can buy beans at a uniform price at the grocery store. A public project that produced cans of beans would therefore evaluate each and every can at the going market price. But there are exceptions. There are types of benefits, such as time saved on the journey to work, for which people put different valuations on the same service. A rich man would pay more than a poor man for the saving of 15 minutes on the journey to work. Marginal evaluations are not equalized because it is physically impossible for a rich man and poor man to trade time at a single price. It follows, therefore, that a strict interpretation of the rules of cost-benefit analysis requires a saving of 15 minutes of a rich man's time to be counted as a greater benefit than a saving of 15 minutes of a poor man's time, even if both savings are procured by expenditure in the public sector and are distributed without cost to the ultimate beneficiaries.

One's feeling of unease about this implication of cost-benefit analysis is magnified when we pass from time-saving to life-saving. A rich man would typically pay more than a poor man to avoid a small probability of losing his life, as for instance when a rich man installs special fire prevention equipment in his house or buys safety devices for his car that a poor man feels he cannot afford. The standard rule in cost-benefit analysis that public evaluation should follow private evaluation would therefore lead the planner to place a higher value on the saving of a life in the design of airports than in the design of roads, because users of airports are, on average, richer than users of roads and would themselves be prepared to pay more to avoid a small probability of losing their lives. The public sector ought, in other words, to place a higher value on the saving of the life of a rich man than on the saving of the life of a poor man because that is what the private sector is, on the whole, inclined to do. Most readers would, I think, object to this rule, especially in view of the fact that life-saving in publicly-financed medical expenditure entails, or ought to entail, no such bias. In preventing the spread of an epidemic, no town, region or person should be favoured over another because one is wealthy while the other is not. What we have here is a conflict between the cost-benefit principle and the equality principle. The former would seem to apply to public projects; the latter would seem to apply to the saving of lives, and a conflict becomes unavoidable in the saving of lives in public projects. I see no resolution of this conflict other than for the citizen to decide which of the conflicting principles of public sector equity takes precedence in any particular case.

The decision to end the draft in the United Sates after the Vietnam War can be looked upon, in part, as a substitution of capitalist equity for the lottery principle as a means of maintaining manpower for the army. Instead of picking soldiers by lot from the appropriate cohort, it was decided to hire soldiers as workers are hired in any branch of the civil service. The issue was complicated by the fact that the lottery principle had not, hitherto, been strictly applied – the upper classes were one way or another evading the worst of military service – but the conflict among systems of equity was important none the less.

There is a constant tension among the principles of merit, equality and capitalist equity in the provision of higher education. The conflict is dealt with, in France, by having two systems of higher education, one open to all and the other restricted by stiff entrance examinations. In the American system of higher education, the merit principle would seem to be dominant in determining admission to the state universities where the fees are very low, while merit and capitalist equity together determine entrance to the private schools, and the principle of equality has a role to play in affirmative action programs designed to give an edge to members of otherwise disadvantaged minority groups.

Conflicts among systems of public sector equity have their counter-parts in conflicts among groups of people likely to be favoured by the different systems. On the issue of life-saving expenditures, the poor naturally favour the equality principle while the rich favour the rigorous application of cost-benefit analysis. In the provision of higher education, the clever students favour the merit principle, the rich would like to see students charged the full cost of their education, and members of min-ority groups naturally support the equality principle in affirmative action. Whether such conflicts are likely to endanger democracy depends on how greatly people are affected by the choice of one system over another. This, in turn, probably depends on the size of the public sector. If the public sector is small, the frequency of conflict among systems of equity is likely to be small as well, for the domains of application of the different systems are unlikely to overlap. As the public sector grows, the frequency of conflict among systems of public sector equity grows accordingly, leading, in the limit, to the problems of democracy under socialism dis-cussed in the last chapter.

These problems become particularly acute if the principles of public sector equity are not strictly applied. For the average man, his education is his most valuable property. His earning power over his life depends more on the number of years of schooling he receives and on the nature of his education (whether he studies medicine or bookkeeping) than on the amount of money or property he inherits. To assign education on the principle of equality or the principle of merit is to remove education from the list of things that money can buy or that a father can transmit directly to his son. Whether, or to what extent, this attenuates the feasibility of capitalist equity depends on how rigorously the principles of equality or merit are applied. Even when these principles are applied strictly, there may be some conflict over the amount of education sup-plied to each child and the weights to be attached to the principles of merit and equality in deciding how total expenditure on education is to be apportioned between bright children, average children and disadvan-taged children. The experience of most countries is that these issues can be resolved amicably. Serious problems begin to arise when the equality or merit principles are not completely respected, when, as is the case in many countries, the race, religion or political affiliation of citizens is taken into account. Children of party members are given priority in education in Russia and China. Children of Malays are given priority over children of Chinese in Malaysia. Much of the conflict over language rights in Quebec has to do with the access to educational opportunity of the non-French population; the requirement to conduct one's elementary and secondary education in French reduces one's chances of acquiring higher education in English without providing, in the estimation of the potential recipients, an equal opportunity for higher education in French.

The general dependence of the feasibility of public sector equity on the scope of the public sector may be seen most clearly in the cost-benefit analysis. Most people are probably prepared to live with the implications of cost-benefit analysis if its range of application is limited to roads, bridges, public buildings, airports, harbors, dams and a few other types of public works. Each man reasons that he will probably benefit in the long run, that the net gain or loss will not constitute a large proportion of his income, and that he is, in any case, better off if the rules of cost-benefit analysis are followed than he would be if each project were undertaken or not according to the degree of political support that could be mustered in its favour. The aggravation and loss of time in political activity would outweigh the advantages he can expect. Better let the planner follow the rules of cost-benefit analysis than risk opening the Pandora's box of political influence upon the choice of projects in the public sector. It is different when the scope of public sector activity is increased. If the planner is to decide in detail what investments are to take place, which regions are to grow and which to decline, and, by implication, who is to prosper and who is not, I had better do what I can to ensure that my interests are attended to, for I can be confident that pressure is being exerted on the planner from all quarters and that I will lose out in the final decision if I let matters take their course.

In short, any government activity requires some political influence on the assignment of income, the extent of that influence is limited by standards of public sector equity, standards of public sector equity conflict with one another, and the acceptability of the different standards becomes progressively weaker as the size and scope of the public sector expands. There is a line beyond which the public sector cannot be expanded if democratic government is to be preserved. It is difficult to say where the line is to be drawn, especially as the effect of public sector activity on the standard of equity depends essentially on what, as well as on how much, the government chooses to do. We shall return to this problem in the final chapter of the book.

THE INCOMPLETE TENURE OF PROPERTY

There can be no capitalist equity without security of property. The problem of faction and the resulting breakdown of democracy through conflict over the assignment of income described in Chapter 2 cannot be avoided in a capitalist economy — indeed, an economy cannot be said to be capitalist at all — if property is insecure, for the squabble over the assignment of property is every bit as corrosive to democracy as the squabble over the assignment of income. It makes no difference whether people fight over the fruit or the tree. With property, as with income, it is unnecessary that feasibility be complete. The government may influence the ascription of property rights to some extent, may redistribute a good deal, and may modify the content of property rights without, at the same time, endangering democratic government. With property, as with income, a degree of feasibility may be traded off for efficiency or for a greater acceptability of the system as a whole. But there are limits beyond which the security and rights of property cannot be attenuated.

Capitalism is a perfectly and completely feasible system of equity in the model of perfect competition because the model, on most formulations, takes no account of the transmission of property from one generation to another, because property is assumed to be completely secure, and because the rights of property are well specified and invariant over time. Complications arising from inheritance are avoided by specifying the basic unit of analysis to be the immortal family rather than the mortal individual. All property is assigned to families. Property, once obtained, may be held indefinitely or until exchanged for another form of property or for consumption goods. As there is no public sector in the model, there can be no question of how to share the tax burden and the rent of publicly owned property, or of using the legislature to redistribute property rights.

Real capitalism, as opposed to the model of perfect competition, is less than completely feasible as a system of equity, not only because of monopoly and government, but because the rights that property is allowed to convey are established in the legislature and are subject to revision at the margin in response to changes in circumstances in the economy and in society at large. In particular, the legislature has to specify the rules of inheritance, the scope of the public sector, the limits of property and contract, and the line between the rights of property and the right each man enjoys by virtue of his status as a citizen.

The rules of inheritance are a compromise between our aversion to the intergenerational transmission of inequality and the requirements of the institution of property. On the one hand, we feel that each man should rise or fall in society, should become rich or poor, as a consequence of his own efforts, and not because family wealth or influence is used on his behalf. People in each generation are like runners in a race, who should win or lose on their own merits. Taken to extreme, this point of view would lead us to prohibit the inheritance of property altogether and to forbid anyone from taking special care over the education of his children. On the other hand, there is reason to believe that the enforcement of starting equality in each generation would be inconsistent with the maintenance of a capitalist economy. No one would accumulate property beyond what he expects to need for his retirement unless a fraction of one's property can be passed down to his children. This conflict of aims lies behind the imposition of an inheritance or estate tax at a rate high enough to moderate the capacity of the wealthy in the present generation to transmit advantages to their children, but not so high as to stifle accumulation altogether.

The scope of the public sector may be specified more or less extensively, the rich generally preferring to limit the 'agenda' and the poor generally preferring to expand it. The agenda is defined as the list of activities undertaken by the public sector. Within the agenda, choices are made in accordance with the mixture of principles described above. Outside the agenda, capitalist equity is the sole principle on which income is assigned. Some items, notably the army, the police and the legislature, are obviously on the agenda because they cannot be provided in the market; others, such as the public school system, are generally believed to belong on the agenda though there are voices of dissent; and still other items are genuinely on the margin with no overwhelming majority either for or against their inclusion. Medicine is in this last category. Medical services are fully on the agenda in the United Kingdom, are paid for by the state but supplied privately in Canada, and are paid for by the state for the old and the poor in the United States. Among the considerations in deciding if medicine belongs on the agenda is whether medical care should be assigned according to the principle of equality or the principle of capitalist equity, whether medical services should be available to everybody as part of their rights as citizens or should be treated as a commodity of which one may purchase as much or as little as he desires or can afford. A similar conflict arises over the assignment of the right of access to parks, beaches and wilderness areas. The right of access to a beach may be made available to all, or the beach may be treated no differently from farmland or residential property that may be privately owned and reserved for the exclusive use of its owner.

A large portion of the property in most capitalist countries is owned by the state. Publicly owned property includes roads, schools, hospitals, land in the public domain (with mineral deposits contained there), and assets of public corporations. There is also a sense in which half of all privately owned corporations is really publicy owned because half the profit accrues to the state in the corporate income tax. Public property in itself need not diminish the feasibility of the capitalist system of equity if the property is used to provide services already on the agenda or if the revenue from the property accrues to the public sector as a substitute for taxation. Public property becomes troublesome, as will be discussed in Chapter 6, if it may be used to influence the assignment of incomes in the private sector.

The rights of property and the rights of people to exchange property and the services of property are never unlimited. My right to do what I please with my property does not extend to the building of a swimming pool inadequately fenced to keep out young children passing by. My right to buy time for television advertising does not extend to using that time for advertising cigarettes. My right to produce what I please with the resources I own or hire does not extend to the production of substances deemed to be dangerous. My right to hire labour does not extend to the hiring of children during school hours. My right to the income from the resources I own does not extend to the point where I can withhold income from people who are actually starving. (Admittedly, this last qualification makes sense only in a society rich enough that starvation is a rare event; otherwise it would make civilisation impossible.) My right, and that of my employee, to decide between us upon the content of the job does not extend to allowing people to work in circumstances deemed by the law to be needlessly and excessively dangerous. My right as an employer does not, in some circumstances at least, permit me to exercise my authority over my employee maliciously or to dismiss him except for reasons having to do with the effectiveness of the firm as a profit-making enterprise.

This last qualification to the rights of property is important but double-edged. It is important because the self-respect of the worker, which contributes both to his well-being and to his effectiveness as a citizen, is diminished if he is at the mercy of every whim of his boss. It is double-edged because extensive job security for the employed may create extensive insecurity for the unemployed or for those engaged in marginal occupations. The greatest defence of the self-respect of labour and the greatest assurance of mutual respect between employer and employee is the knowledge that a man who resigns or is dismissed from one job can easily find another. Too much or too extensive job security imposed by law or by powerful trade unions may actually diminish the status of the worker by tying him to a particular job, though a moderate security against wilful or arbitrary dismissal may have the opposite effect.

The rights of property and the rights of citizens tend to overlap and conflict in all of the circumstances we have been examining, but the most direct and immediate conflict arises over political activity itself. We do not allow citizens to buy or sell votes, and we are uneasy about the use of wealth to control the means of communication or to finance political parties. People differ in their opinions as to where the line should be drawn. Some are sanguine about the role of wealth in politics. They would finance political parties from private contributions alone, place no limit or disclosure rules on such contributions, refrain from any provision of time on television or space in newspapers to political parties over and above what the parties are prepared to pay for, and prohibit campaigning or mass demonstrations except in halls specifically hired for the purpose. Others seek to limit and circumscribe the political power of wealth on the grounds that office ought not to be among the goods that money can buy. They would be inclined to limit the amount of private contributions to political parties, supply political parties public funds in accordance with their voting strength, and permit use of streets and public places in campaigning.

Though there must be a minimal specification of property rights below which capitalism ceases to serve as a prerequisite to democracy, the general argument connecting capitalism and democracy gives little guidance as to where to draw the line between the rights of citizens and the rights of property — that is, between the rights of citizens as voters and the rights of citizens as property owners. Externalities are sometimes relevant; certain usages of property may be prohibited because of their effects on third parties or on the population as a whole. The state sometimes protects people from their own foolishness. Limitation of the rights of property may make capitalism more acceptable to the poor or the unlucky.

Some conservative thinkers have tried to circumvent the issue by an appeal to freedom as an ultimate value. If you believe in freedom, so the argument goes, then you must want the widest possible extension of the rights of property, limited only by the degree of coercion required to finance and administer public goods such as the army and the police. I am more free if I spend as much or as little of my money as I please on the education of my children than if the government takes away a part of my money and provides my children with the sort of education it thinks fit; and I should, in my own interest, advocate that education be provided in the private sector rather than in the public sector of the economy. Similarly, I should object to regulations obliging riders of motorcycles to wear helmets, to restrictions on sales or advertisements of heroin, and, of course, to any form of public provision of medical care.

This argument is buttressed by two others to which it is, in a general way, related. The first is that economic freedom is not only of value in itself but is necessary as a prerequisite to democracy. Abolish economic freedom and, regardless of one's wishes in the matter, political freedom will sooner or later be abolished as well. The second is semantic. Not only is economic freedom required for political freedom, but they are two sides of the same coin, bound together because they are made of the same stuff. One need only ask oneself how to draw the line between economic and political freedom and it at once becomes evident that no such line exists. Restrictions on emigration would normally be thought of as being in the domain of political freedom, and currency restrictions would normally be thought of as being in the domain of economic freedom, but restrictions on currency for the purchase of boat or aeroplane tickets can prevent emigration as effectively as its outright prohibition. Similarly, prohibition of certain types of advertising shades imperceptibly into the prohibition of free speech.

Let us consider these arguments in the reverse of the order in which they have been presented. The semantic argument we can almost reject out of hand. Society uses many distinctions with no clear line of demarcation between extremes. We distinguish between manslaughter and murder, though examples can be produced of acts that are neither wholly one nor wholly the other; the law recognizes the existence of the crime of murder despite the fact that there are acts of which it cannot be said with confidence whether they are murder or not. Nor are we inclined to give up the distinction between bonds and money merely because there are financial instruments that are neither wholly bonds nor wholly money. It is enough that there are some instruments we are inclined to classify as bonds but not money, and other instruments we are inclined to classify as money but not bonds. As for economic freedom and political freedom, it is enough that we can produce examples that are either one or the other, for instance, the right to use one's money to buy diamonds and the right to vote, and we need not give up the distinction merely because there are instances where both freedoms are involved at once.

With the other subordinate argument, that economic freedom is a prerequisite to political freedom, I can hardly disagree, for a large part of this book is devoted to making precisely that point. But there is a crucial distinction between 'all' and 'some'. Some economic freedom – perhaps a great deal – is certainly necessary, and one can imagine property rights being pared down to the point where capitalism can no longer be said to exist, or where the economic prerequisite to democracy is absent altogether. It does not follow from this line of argument that all economic freedom – or all policies alleged to enhance economic freedom – is necessary or desirable. One of the main themes of this book – that it is sometimes appropriate to modify pure capitalism to make the resulting system acceptable to the great majority of voters — can be restated as the proposition that democracy is strengthened if certain types of economic freedom are curtailed. Economic freedom may be restricted to some extent to place a floor on how much a man stands to lose under capitalism if he is unsuccessful in the market. The freedom to buy votes or to sell oneself into slavery would, in all probability, destroy democracy by creating a class of desperate men with an incentive to overthrow the institutions of society. We shall return to this point in our discussion of the acceptability of capitalism.

Against the main argument — that we wish to maximize the scope of property rights because freedom is the goal of economic and political activity — I would be inclined to deny the major premise altogether. Freedom, as an undifferentiated entity, is not the sole end of economic and political activity. There are other goals, namely prosperity and equality; and the word freedom is a cover term for many particular freedoms, some of which are very important and some not. Freedom of speech, freedom to move from one part of the country to another, to change jobs and to vote are very important; freedom to choose among many varieties of shirts or motorcars is of some value; freedom of my children to see heroin advertised on television as safe and enjoyable is a freedom I would prefer not to have at all. Some economic freedoms are valuable for their own sake, others are necessary as a prerequisite to democracy, still others are dispensible altogether. The case for preserving or not preserving any particular instance of economic freedom has to be made on its own merits.

There is a strong economic case for not restricting economic freedom too much, a case that has nothing to do with the preservation of democracy except in so far as prosperity is itself conducive to democracy. It is simply that a man is better off if he himself spends a given sum of money on what he values most than if the state spends it on his behalf. The restriction of the scope of what money can buy is normally coupled with a decision by the state to supply whatever it is that money is not allowed to buy, and the supply is usually either the same for everyone or as much as each man wants to take, elementary education being an example of the former and socialized medicine being an example of the latter. A man is better off if he himself can decide how much he wishes to spend on these commodities, either more or less than the state would supply on his behalf depending on his taste for the product. This is true to some extent even for regulations on matters such as work safety; the worker could choose to work in a safe shop where wages are relatively low or in a risky one where wages are relatively high.

The efficiency argument for the extension of economic freedom is strengthened if society redistributes income substantially or if the ownership of human and non-human wealth is widely dispersed, for in that case the principal motive for reducing the scope of the rights of property — namely to lessen social conflict by narrowing the gap in the standards of living of the rich and poor and reducing the extent to which the wealthy can transmit their advantages to the next generation — loses much of its force. It is less important, for instance, to have elementary education in the public sector in a society where everyone is more or less equal in status and where the different private schools would reflect different religions of the parents (as long as religion has no political significance) or different views about how children should be educated, than it would be in a society with great differences in wealth and status where the school system is used — as it is in England — to perpetuate a class structure from one generation to the next.

The determination of the limits of property rights is a balancing of considerations, many of which are difficult or impossible to quantify: the advantage of being able to buy as much of each commodity as one's demands for other goods will allow, the need to preserve capitalism as a prerequisite to democracy, the effect of extending the advantages of wealth on the acceptability of capitalism, and technical considerations having to do with the incompleteness of the average citizen's knowledge of the safety of products offered for sale. The balancing of these and other considerations is necessarily a political judgement. There is no shortcut via the maximization of freedom. Blanket arguments about maximizing freedom can lead to the advocacy of social and economic policies detrimental to democracy and to freedom itself.

There is also a political, or rhetorical, reason for avoiding the simple argument that all economic freedom is a requirement for the maintenance of democracy. The support of capitalism has to be distinguished from the support of capitalists. In a capitalist society, the wealthy, the well-connected and the managers of large chunks of the nation's means of production have an incentive to extend the rights of property in every possible direction, just as the poor and powerless have an incentive to see the rights of property circumscribed. Any defence of capitalism is therefore suspect, especially if the defender is himself wealthy or obviously dependent on the goodwill of the wealthy. The privileged have always defended their privileges as necessary for the common good. No defence of capitalism can ever be entirely free of the taint of self-interest, but no defence of capitalism can be generally persuasive unless it speaks to the poor as well as to the rich. The problem is to show why a poor man should, in his own interest, respect the rules despite the fact that he is poor and that capitalism seems more beneficial to his neighbours than to himself. It is, therefore, particularly important not to debase the argument about capitalism and democracy by pushing it farther than is absolutely necessary. The defence of capitalism is, at least to some extent, the defence of privilege,[10] and to defend privilege beyond the point where it is necessary for democracy and prosperity is to run the risk of having the whole argument rejected as a fraud.

THE ACCEPTABILITY OF CAPITALISM

Acceptability, as the term is used in this book, is not a moral criterion. To ask whether capitalism is acceptable is not to ask whether it is desirable on certain principles, whether I like it, whether the reader ought to approve of it, or even whether the majority of voters should be inclined to favour it. Acceptability, as the term is used here, is akin to the concept of stability. An organism or structure is said to be stable if it does not fall apart, if it maintains itself over time. A proposed system of equity is acceptable, regardless of its desirability on ethical or other grounds, if no majority of voters can be found to overthrow it, and it is unacceptable otherwise.

An example may clarify the meaning of the term. Consider once again the model society from Chapter 2 where $300,000 a year is apportioned among 15 men, and suppose our citizens like to take chances. Each citizen would get $20,000 if the national income were divided up equally, but five citizens could each receive $40,000 if the remaining 10 citizens received only $10,000 each. It is conceivable that the citizens could agree among themselves to divide the national income unequally, five people getting $40,000 and 10 people getting $10,000 per year, on the understanding that the five people to receive the high incomes would be chosen by lot. The citizens reach this agreement because, being gamblers at heart, they prefer a small chance of a large income to a certainty of a smaller one as long as the expected value of income is the same in each case. To make the example very strong, let us suppose that the lottery is run once and for all and that each man's income is high or low forever after, according to the outcome of the lottery.

Assignment by lottery is fair in the sense that all citizens agree to it in advance; it is unacceptable as the term is used here because it is unenforceable. The ten losers have lost income but they have not lost the vote, and there is nothing to prevent them from using their majority in the legislature to reestablish equality or to expropriate the five winners altogether. The day after the lottery, the losers overturn the result; or their children do so, claiming with considerable justification that they never agreed to the lottery and will not be bound by the foolishness or immorality of their elders. Furthermore, if all citizens understand the dynamics of their own society and know, in advance, what the full consequences of assignment of income by lottery would be, they will, each of them, refuse to assign income by lot even though each citizen would accept the gamble if the outcome could be enforced. Acceptability, as defined here, is not a consequence of the volition of the average voter. It is a consequence of interactions among voters. Assignment by lot is not accepted because it is unacceptable — not the other way around.

A method of assignment of income is defined as acceptable if there is always a majority of voters, each member of which believes himself better off in the long run than he would be under any alternative method of assignment. He may hold that belief for a variety of reasons and may interpret himself to be 'better off' in a more or less altruistic way. He may prefer a society without great disparities of income and wealth, not only because he is concerned that he or his children may end up among the poor, but because he feels uncomfortable knowing there is poverty around him, and would happily sacrifice some of his own income to see the worst of poverty eliminated. Similarly, slavery may be unacceptable to one whose own income would be higher in a society with slavery than in a society where slavery is prohibited. But, in judging the acceptability of a method of assignment, a good deal of weight should be attached to narrowly selfish considerations. Each voter may be thought of as constantly asking himself whether he would be more prosperous, whether he would have a more satisfying job, or whether he would have greater respect in the community under a different method of assignment. Only if the majority of voters can answer these questions in the negative — only if the majority thinks itself better off on the whole under the existing system than it would be under any conceivable alternative, another system of equity or a method of political assignment — can the existing system be said to be acceptable.

Is capitalism acceptable in this sense? One might claim that capitalism is obviously acceptable because it exists. The power of the vote may be used to abolish capitalism at any time. That capitalism has not been overturned must mean that it is acceptable to a majority of voters who think themselves better off under capitalism than they would otherwise be. While this justification of the acceptability of capitalism is not altogether wrong, it is not entirely dependable, because voters may be mistaken and may come, in time, to realize their mistake, or because underlying technical and social conditions may be changing in such a way that capitalist assignment, which was once acceptable, will soon cease to be so. Just as any social institution may persist through inertia long after it has ceased to be useful, so capitalism may persist after it has ceased to be acceptable. Prior to reform, there must be a moment when the institution to be reformed is unwanted despite the fact that it is there, and the length of time between the moment when the institution becomes unsuitable and the moment when it is reformed may be long or short according to the circumstances. One cannot rule out *a priori* the possibility that capitalism itself has outlived its usefulness and will, in time, be replaced.

It is arguable, for instance, that a viable alternative to capitalism has become possible only with the development of high-speed computers and improved means of communication in the last few years. The argument is that the alternative to capitalism is socialism, that socialism requires central direction of the economy, and that central direction of the economy, which would have been unacceptably inefficient before the new means of communication were developed, is no longer so. Capitalism, though it has not yet been dismantled, is no longer acceptable because a viable socialist alternative has emerged. I do not wish to discuss the substance of the argument here, because the possibility of a socialist equity has already been examined in Chapter 4 and because the efficiency of socialism is outside the scope of this book. All I wish to show by the argument is that the acceptability of capitalism cannot be presumed. To show that capitalism is acceptable we need to demonstrate that a majority of voters has an interest in its continuance.

What we call capitalism is a set of institutions continually changing in ways that are, to some extent, though not entirely, controllable. We want to know precisely why capitalism is acceptable in order to predict the effects on the acceptability of capitalism of changes in technology, economic organization and economic policy. One of the central propositions of the book is that capitalism is the only more or less feasible, more or less acceptable, system of equity — the only method of assignment consistent with democracy in the long run. If that is so, it becomes of the greatest importance to know which sorts of economic policy are likely to reinforce the system of equity and which are likely to attenuate it. It is not sufficient for this purpose that a change in economic institutions be acceptable in the simple sense that voters approve of it. What is relevant is the effect of the policy on voters' acceptance of capitalism as a whole. The example at the outset of this chapter is instructive on this point, for the consequences of the lottery were unacceptable though the lottery itself was not.

There is, in fact, a strong reason why capitalism ought *not* to be acceptable. It ought not to be acceptable because the equality of citizens as voters is in flat contradiction to their inequality of income, wealth and inherited status in the community. Why do people who are politically equal, and who take it as a matter of faith that each man is a good as the next, with equal obligations to the community and equal rights to whatever society has to offer — why do such people tolerate a society where some are allowed to start out with substantial advantages not available to the rest? Why should a poor man, born in a slum, deprived of the advantages of travel and experience available to children of the rich, badly educated in local schools because his parents were unable to afford to move into a neighbourhood with good schools or to send him to a private school, denied entrance to university, and without the capital, contacts or the extraordinary ability required to start a business for himself — why should such a man not band together with other poor men to vote for the overthrow of a system that puts them at such a disadvantage? The income distribution is always skewed so that most people earn less than the average income. (This is no paradox; in a five-man community where the incomes are $10,000, $12,000, $14,000, $16,000 and $30,000, the average income is $16,400 though all but one man earns less than that amount). Why should not the poorer half of the community form a political party to eliminate the privileges of the rich?

The situation is, in some respects, like that in the assignment by lottery discussed at the beginning of this section, where the poorer members of the new generation feel no obligation to abide by the original contract. They never agreed to it. Men who are born poor cannot be said, in any relevant sense, to have had an equal chance of being born rich. They do not even have the satisfaction of supposing that their parents particpated in a lottery. Some wealth is undoubtedly the consequence of industry on the part of the man who accumulated it, but some is nothing more than the loot of a thief passed on to his children and legitimized through continuous possession.

We have to recognize and make full allowance for the contradiction between the equality of citizens as voters and their inequalities of wealth, for any defence of capitalism that denies or belittles this fact is destined to be shallow and unpersuasive. What has to be shown, if capitalism is to be proved acceptable, is that it is in the long run in the interest of the poor to acquiesce to the privilege of the rich. A substantial majority of those whose incomes and inherited privileges are below the average in the community must, as it were, say to themselves: I know I got a poor deal in the portion the capitalist system assigned me at birth, but I will not attempt to right the wrong because there is no way to do so without making myself and my children worse off in the end.

We must be careful with this argument. It cannot be a blanket objection to reform of any kind. There may be ways to reduce disparities of inherited wealth without bringing on a greater degree of political assignment of income than is consistent with the continuance of democracy, and if such reforms can be identified, they should be supported by one whose first concern is to preserve the economic prerequisite to democracy. Whether or not one wants to call the economy so reformed by the name of capitalism is immaterial, though we are, in fact, using the term capitalism to cover forms of economic organization that may differ considerably from the textbook model of perfect competition.

There are three reasons why capitalism is likely to be acceptable in the sense that the great majority of voters, those who are poor as well as those who are rich, have an incentive to preserve some form of capitalist economic organization: (1) capitalism is the only form of economic organization consistent with democracy in a large complex society, (2) capitalism has been the occasion of enormous material prosperity, and (3) the spread between incomes of rich and poor and the barriers to intergenerational mobility are small by comparison with most other societies.

The first we have already discussed, though the statement above goes farther than we have actually proved. We have shown that perfect competition is perfectly feasible as a system of equity, and we have claimed that the degree of equity in many capitalist countries is sufficient for the maintenance of democratic government. We have not shown capitalism to be the only possible system of equity, but we have argued that socialism will not do, and a case can be made that other candidates, such as the corporate state, will not do either. The argument here is that capitalism is acceptable *because* it is feasible, and because there is no other feasible method for assigning incomes to people prior to and independently of decisions of government or legislature. A man who favours democracy must therefore support a bare minimum of private ownership and control of the means of production, for the alternative is socialism, which we know is not feasible.

The second rests on a particular interpretation of the economic history of the last few hundred years. There is no denying that this era has seen a rise in living standards in Europe and America unique in the history of the world. A child born today in the worst poverty and the least favourable circumstances we know in Europe and America has a substantially greater expectation of life than a child of a king or nobleman at any time in history up to the turn of this century. We have enough to eat; we are properly clothed; the great majority of people have a reasonable amount of living space; we are no longer so burdened with hard work that we lack time or energy for leisure and recreation; our standards of sanitation are unprecedented; and most people can afford holidays across continents or across the world. Kings and emperors of the past may have enjoyed greater luxury, but they could not travel as we do or communicate over long distances, and they suffered pain, injury and disease that medical science enables us to avoid.

What is debatable is whether capitalism was a necessary condition for all this to have come about. A strong case can be made for the proposition that the greater part of the prosperity we enjoy in Europe and America, and which would, most likely, be enjoyed in the rest of the world as well if the potential were not dissipated in population growth, is a direct consequence of the advancement of science, and would have come under almost any form of economic organization as long as the advancement of science proceeded as it did. We are prosperous now because we can do things we have never been able to do before, and our increased power over nature has been acquired not in the boardrooms of corporations, but in our research laboratories.

Nor can the advancement of science be thought of as a direct and simple outcome of capitalist economic organization. Scientific knowledge has accumulated gradually over millenia and in a great variety of political regimes and forms of economic organization. Even in a capitalist society, much of the basic research in science and medicine has been conducted in government laboratories and in universities financed by the public sector. Research now conducted in the private sector might be financed and motivated differently, especially as research has become institutionalized and the independent inventor has given way to the large research establishment that, one suspects, would carry on its work much the same in the public as in the private sector. Perhaps capitalism was necessary for the advancement of science at a certain stage of its evolution when the connection between invention and profitability was direct and immediate, but is no longer necessary now that science has built up a momentum of its own.

The defence of capitalism as the occasion of the enormous economic growth we have enjoyed need not belittle the role of the advancement of science or deny that scientific progress is raising the standard of living. It may be sufficient to recall that the profit motive has encouraged and continues to encourage certain types of discoveries, and that capitalism did not impede the government's activity in basic research. It is, I think, significant that the development of mass production of consumer goods, the invention of most new types of consumer goods and much of the world's basic research has been undertaken in capitalist countries, while the one area where the Soviet Union seems to be holding its own is in the development and production of military equipment. The connection between capitalism and prosperity may be indirect. It may be, for all we know, that democracy is now the real requirement for the advancement of science, and that capitalism enters the story as a prerequisite for democracy rather than as a direct prerequisite for continued scientific progress. Democracy, science, capitalism and material prosperity have emerged together in the last few hundred years; the removal of any of these four pillars of the modern world may lead to the collapse of the other three.

The third reason why capitalism is likely to be acceptable has to do with the extent of inequality of income and wealth. We have argued that any inequality tends to undermine capitalism as a method of assignment because inequality is a standing temptation to the poor to expropriate the rich. (Expropriation is perhaps the wrong word here, for it carries overtones of one party taking from another what rightfully belongs to the latter. From the assumption of individualistic communism in the first chapter, it follows that there are no ultimate, God-given property rights, or, if there are, that they are of no interest to us here.) The question is whether the unavoidable inequality in a capitalist economy can be kept from provoking a majority of voters to replace capitalism with another form of economic organization. The inequality of capitalism need not be translated into hostile political action as long as most voters feel that inequality would be greater still in any conceivable alternative, that general prosperity would be adversely affected if capitalism were abolished, or that democracy itself is at stake. In evaluating proposals for economic policy or major changes in economic organization, each voter must draw a balance between what he stands to gain (or lose, as the case may be) from the reassignment or redistribution of income, against what he stands to lose (or gain) from effects upon the general prosperity or the quality of political life. In this calculation, the potential gain from reassignment increases with the size of the spread between the incomes of rich and poor, and the probability of the poor attempting to reassign income through a change in economic organization increases accordingly.

Much depends on whether the trend of capitalism is towards ever greater equality or the reverse. If the trend is towards equality, the incentive to reassign income is automatically less than it would otherwise be because part of what might be gained from reassignment can be gained costlessly by waiting, and because the man at the low end of the income distribution knows that his son has an excellent chance of being substantially better off than he. But if the distribution of income is becoming steadily less equal and if, as Marx claimed, there is in capitalism an inevitable and irresistible separation of people into two opposing classes, owners and workers, with less and less contact between them and an ever-widening disparity in their incomes – then it becomes unlikely, almost impossible, for democracy to continue because workers with the political power to displace the capitalist class will eventually be inclined to do so, and the capitalists or their successors will, at that point, abolish democracy to preserve their privileged position. Democracy would not be viable, in these circumstances, for precisely the reason it was alleged not to be viable in the feudal organization of society in the Middle Ages.

An example may help at this point. Imagine an economy in which the average income is $100 and where the effect of a reassignment — which may be thought of as the replacement of capitalism with another form of economic organization — would reduce average income to $80. If each man feels he has an equal chance of being rich or poor under the proposed reassignment, then any man whose income under the existing arrangements is less than $80 will favour the change and any man whose income is above $80 will oppose it. In a five-man community, the present arrangement will be preserved if the incomes are $70, $90, $100, $110 and $130, but it will be overthrown if they are $60, $60, $70, $125 and $125. And, if redistribution can be effected costlessly, it would be in the interest of the two richest men in the latter case to agree to redistribute to the point where a majority of voters have incomes of $80 or above.

The trend toward or against equality is difficult to describe because equality is multidimensional and because the statistical evidence is affected by anti-poverty policy. When speaking of the trend of equality, one might refer to changes in the percentage of the population above some arbitrarily given poverty line, the shares of income accruing to the different quintiles of the population, the share of wealth accruing to the top, say, 1 per cent of wealth-holders, the intergenerational mobility of the population from one social class to another, or the concentration of control of the economy in a small number of hands.

There is no doubt that the growth of real national income per head has tended to eliminate poverty. For any poverty line whatever, the proportion of the Canadian or American population below that line has steadily diminished for as far back in this century as the data allow us to see. The poverty line most frequently referred to in government reports and public discussion is a level of real income at which a typical family faced with 1965 prices would be inclined to spend a third of its income on food (this signifies a level of real income, because the share of income spent on food declines systematically as income rises). In the United States, the incidence of poverty, on this definition, has decreased[11] from 17.3 per cent of the population in 1959 to 3.0 per cent of the population in 1975. The decline is due in part to the general rise in real income over these years, and in part to the expansion of the welfare programme — the introduction of food stamps in 1964, the introduction of public medical care for the old in 1965, and the general increase in benefits from unemployment insurance and social security.

The alleviation of poverty through an extensive programme of transfers to the poor might be rejected as evidence of the long-run propensity of capitalism because the introduction of transfers is a movement away from pure capitalism towards a different system of assignment, or because it is inequality rather than poverty that renders capitalism unacceptable. The first point is essentially semantic. Whether one wants to reserve the term 'capitalism' for an economy without transfers or to use the term to describe the economy as it has evolved in Europe and America is a matter of definition, not of analysis. The important question is whether a system of transfers imposed upon an otherwise capitalist economy is likely to be corrosive of democracy. We shall return to this question in the next chapter.

The second point is probably right. The number of people in poverty may well be irrelevant to the stability of democracy. (How many of the citizens of ancient Athens enjoyed a standard of living in excess of what we now call the poverty line?) What counts is the spread between the incomes of rich and poor, for the percentage by which the poor can expect their incomes to increase in a reassignment depends on the dispersion of the income distribution, regardless of whether the absolute income of, say, the poorest 20 per cent is large or small. The evidence is difficult to interpret because it is not always clear how to make allowances for the impact on families of the different, partly overlapping, transfer programmes, for the public expenditure on education, for changes in the composition of the family as the birth rate declines and progressively more old people choose to live alone, for the normal change in a man's income over his life cycle[12] (income is low at first, rises to a peak when a man is in middle age, and declines thereafter), for the fact that some people with low incomes in any given year are not permanently poor (a man whose income is recorded as $3,000 may be desperately poor, or he may be a prosperous businessman experiencing a bad year), and for the effects of taxes on a family's disposable income.[13]

The weight of evidence points to a long-run trend towards modestly greater equality in the distribution of income in most Western countries. The pattern for the United States may be seen in Table 5.2, showing quintile shares from 1926 to 1977 of family income defined inclusive of transfers but with no deduction for income and payroll tax. (For instance, the number 5.2 at the top of the right hand column of the table means that the poorest 20 per cent of the population in 1977 earned only 5.2 per cent of total family income or 26 per cent (5.2 ÷ 20) of what they would have earned if there had been full and complete equality of incomes in the United States at that time.) The trend towards greater equalization has been steady up to the 1970s, when a slight reversal is observed, but the reversal in the statistics may be deceiving for the reasons stated above. More or less the same pattern seems to be observed for inequalities of wealth, as opposed to income, and for inter-

Table 5.2. The distribution of family income in the United States

Quintile shares	1926	1935-36	1941	1950	1960	1970	1977
	%	%	%	%	%	%	%
Lowest	12.5	4.1	4.1	4.5	4.8	5.4	5.2
Second		9.2	9.5	12.0	12.2	12.2	11.6
Third	13.8	14.1	15.3	17.4	17.8	17.6	17.5
Fourth	19.3	20.9	22.3	23.4	24.0	23.8	24.2
Highest	54.4	51.7	48.8	42.7	41.3	40.9	41.5
Share of the top 5%	30.0	26.5	24.0	17.3	15.9	15.6	15.7
Average *per capita* disposable income in constant 1972 dollars	$1,666	$1,607	$2,068	$2,386	$2,697	$3,619	$4,293

Sources: Historical Statistics of the United States, Colonial Times to 1970, United States Department of Commerce, series G319–336 for income shares from 1926 to 1950 and series F19 and F31 for *per capita* income. *Statistical Abstract of the United States 1978,* Table 734 for income shares from 1950 to 1977 and Table 714 for *per capita* income. There does not appear to be a consistent time series of quintile shares over the whole of the period from 1926 to 1977. Instead, there are two overlapping time series with different definitions of family income: 'family personal income' for the earlier period and 'money income of families' for the later period. In the table, statistics for 1950 and beyond are based on money income of families. For comparison, note that quintile shares of family personal income in 1950 were, from lowest to highest, 4.8, 10.9, 16.1, 22.1, and 46.1; the share of the top 5% was 21.5.

generational mobility among social classes. Wealth is, of course, much less equally distributed than income. The evidence is of a decline in the share of total wealth held by the top one-half of one per cent of the population, from about 35 per cent in 1929 to about 25 per cent in 1969, with a levelling off after the Second World War which might be attributed to a decline in personal savings as a consequence of the social security system.[14] Add title to social security payments to the estimate of private wealth, and the distribution becomes more equal than it has ever been before.

In assessing the degree of inequality in contemporary capitalism, one must keep in mind how enormously unequal the distribution of income has been in other societies, and that the main source of great wealth or power has historically been the favour of the king or the leaders of the ruling party rather than success in business. Cardinal Wolsey, the Chancellor of Henry VIII, is said to have acquired property worth £35,000 a year at a time when the annual wage was £6 a year;[15] Wolsey's income exceeded that of an average man by a factor of about 6,000. By contrast, the President of the United States earns $200,000, a mere 13 times the average family income,[16] and the president of a large corporation is unlikely to earn more than a $1 million, or 67 times the average family income.

The history of inequality in Britain is instructive. According to the best evidence we have,[17] the degree of inequality has remained virtually constant for over 200 years from 1688 to 1913, right through the Industrial Revolution and the rise in the general standard of living. Capitalism in Britain did not intensify inequality, but did not reduce it either, until the First World War, after which distribution of income has become steadily more equal year by year. One can see this reflected in the houses of any major city. The most substantial and elegant dwellings are those built by the old nobility, if there were any, or by the prosperous merchants and businessmen of the late nineteenth century. Since then, houses have reflected the democratization of economic life, and the difference between the housing of the rich and the housing of the average family is not as great as it used to be.

There is also a qualitative equalization, over and above what is indicated in the statisitics. Benefits of many new products accrue equally, or almost equally, to everyone. Whether one watches television on a big screen or a little screen, the content is the same for all viewers, and the quality of life for the four-odd hours the average person watches per day is the same whether one is rich or poor. Cars may differ, but the roads and the scenery along the roads are the same for everyone. The diets of the rich and poor, if they differ at all, do so for cultural rather than financial reasons.[18] And one need only contrast the massive May Day parades, the total adulation of the leaders, and the personal demeanour of the leaders of Communist countries with the ordinary ways of prominent men in government and industry under capitalism to appreciate where real and thoroughgoing inequality is to be found. Especially in a rich society, the inequalities that sting are not so much the inequalities of wealth as the inequalities of hierarchy, and it is difficult to see how these inequalities can be anything but increased, magnified and made more painful by the replacement of capitalism with any other system of industrial organization we know.

To sum up, the compatibility of capitalism and democracy depends on the feasibility and acceptability of capitalism: whether capitalism allows enough of each man's income to be determined outside of and independently of the public sector for democracy to be maintained, and whether the rules of assignment of incomes under capitalism are such as voters will be inclined to respect and preserve. The feasibility of capitalism is, as we have shown, far from complete. Monopoly leads to political influence upon the assignment of incomes because government must frequently break the impasse when two monopolies confront one another as in wage bargaining for an entire industry, or because a firm is prevented by the government from taking full advantage of the power to set prices that monopoly would otherwise confer. Any task of government affects the assignment of incomes to some extent. The effect of taxes is direct and immediate, but the assignment of incomes is also affected by the choice of types and quantities of public goods, by public investment in industry, by social security, trade policy, agricultural policy, and so on through the whole list of activities of the public sector. And there is an unavoidable element of political assignment of incomes in the need for the legislature to establish the content of property rights, − to determine what money is allowed to buy and what citizens are to have by right. Societies we call capitalist are not entirely free of political influence upon the apportionment of the national income among citizens, and are, to some extent, subject to political conflict over assignment as described in Chapter 2. I would, none the less, be inclined to speculate that the extent of political assignment in countries like Canada and the United States, though increasing, is not yet so great as to be unmanageable. We can live with a degree of political assignment, and the degree of political assignment today may still be within the limit of what democracy can tolerate.

Whether capitalism will be allowed to continue is another matter altogether. Of the reasons why capitalism might be acceptable to a majority of voters − that capitalism is the only form of economic organization known to be even partially feasible as a system of equity; that capitalism has coincided with the greatest and most sustained rise in the standard of living of the majority of people the world has ever seen; and that the distribution of income is narrow by historical standards − of these reasons, I would be inclined to emphasize the first. It is arguable that capitalism is no longer a requirement for the continuance of economic growth, and that the advancement of science would not be impeded if science and technology were entirely under the auspices of the public sector. It is also arguable that great disparities of income between rich and poor that persist under capitalism could be eliminated through a different form of economic organization. Democracy, on the other hand, which may be the real prerequisite both for continued advancement of science and for the maintenance of a degree of equality in the income distribution, requires that a substantial portion of income be assigned outside the political arena. This requirement cannot, so far as as we can tell, be met except by an economy run more or less on capitalist lines. Capitalism, in other words, is feasible as a system of equity and may be acceptable for that reason alone.

Throughout this chapter, we have reasoned as though the choice were between capitalism as it is and some totally different form of economic organization, the leading candidate being socialism as practised in the Soviet Union or perhaps Yugoslavia. It was as though the Red Banner were raised in Times Square and we had to choose whether to follow it. Sometimes one does have to make such a choice, as, for instance, in the national elections in France and Italy in the mid-1970s, but no such choices have been implicit in elections in the United Kingdom, Canada or the United States. The choices in these latter countries have always been among alternative groups of leaders, economic policies and institutions within a broad framework of capitalism and democracy. Thus, to be useful, our analysis of the economic prerequisite to democracy must be extended from the comparison of large systems of industrial organization to the study of how economic policy might strengthen or attenuate the system of equity. It is to this question that we now turn.

6

The Political Implications of Economic Policy

Poverty is the cause of the defects of democracy. That is the reason why measures should be taken to ensure a permanent level of prosperity. This is in the interest of all classes, including the prosperous themselves; and therefore, the proper policy is to accumulate any surplus revenue in a fund, and then distribute this fund in block grants to the poor . . . to make such grants sufficient for the purchase of a plot of land; failing that, they should be large enough to start men in commerce or agriculture.

Aristotle[1]

The role of equity in economic policy is best discussed in a context where three criteria are recognized: efficiency, equality, and equity itself. The first two are the traditional criteria in formal economic analysis.[2] Efficiency is the maximization of real national income regardless of how the income is apportioned among citizens. Efficiency is the criterion usually applied in cost-benefit analysis for choosing among projects within a circumscribed agenda of activities of the public sector. To recognize equality as a criterion for the evaluation of economic policy is to judge one policy preferable to another if it tends to equalize the distribution of income when the effects on the size of real income are the same; in a three-person economy, a policy that results in incomes of 15, 20 and 25 is therefore preferred, on this criterion, to a policy that results in incomes of 10, 20 and 30. When efficiency and equality are recognized as joint criteria, we require a procedure for deciding which takes precedence or how the two criteria are to be balanced when they conflict. We may construct a rough rule of thumb for weighting equality and efficiency, or we may attempt to subsume them in a single, higher criterion as in classical utilitarianism discussed in connection with planning under socialism in Chapter 4.

The addition of equity as a criterion for the assessment of economic policy is novel in one sense but not in another. It is novel in the sense that equity is almost always ignored in the formal analysis of economic policy. This is clearly so when policy is evaluated by a utilitarian criterion; the total utility in a three-person economy where one man gets $10, a second gets $20 and a third gets $30 is the same regardless of who gets the high income and who gets the low income, and it is unaffected by a reassignment of incomes among the three. It is also the case for most of the alternative criteria that economists have considered. The effect of policy on the solidity of property rights or the viability of democratic government is rarely taken into account, the implicit assumption being that political institutions work well or badly as the case may be regardless of what policy is adopted. Examine the arguments for or against tariffs in a treatise on international trade, or consider the lists of advantages of the different kinds of taxes in a treatise on public finance, and ask, in each case, what criteria are being applied. Almost without exception, the criteria are efficiency, or efficiency and equality together. The connections between policies and their ultimate effects may be complex and roundabout. It may be argued, for instance, that a tariff which under normal circumstances is inefficient is not so in a particular case because it is the only means at hand to correct for distortions in prices or wages in the domestic economy. Or it may be argued that the community is better off on a utilitarian criterion because the beneficiaries of the tariff are poor, the people harmed by the tariff are rich, and there is no practical means for the latter to compensate the former should the tariff be removed. One way or another, the consequences of policies or actions get translated into measures of efficiency or equality, and the policies themselves are evaluated accordingly.

On the other hand — and this is the sense in which the introduction of equity as a criterion is not novel — it is, I believe, quite common for citizens, politicians, judges and even economists to take political consequences of economic policy into account. By political consequences, I do not refer merely to the constraints imposed upon economic policy by the views of politicians and citizens at the moment. I refer to the recognition that certain types of economic policy can provoke political conflict among social classes and can affect the working of democracy adversely, even if these policies are approved by the great majority of the voters. I think — and I hope the discussion in this chapter will bear the view out — that political consequences are recognized informally. Policy-makers do have a sense of when analysis based on the criteria of efficiency and equality should be carried to its logical conclusion, and when other, frequently ill-defined, considerations should be allowed to intervene. Respect for property rights is clearly a consideration of this kind.

It might be supposed that informal recognition of equity is sufficient. As equity is a difficult concept to pin down, and as one cannot calibrate equity in any obviously appropriate way, a case can be made for ignoring equity in the formal analysis of economic policy and introducing it afterward as an informal constraint in policy implementation. The difficulty with such a procedure is that the formal recognition of a criterion and its full incorporation into the analysis of economic policy gives that criterion a definite edge over criteria that are not so recognized. While it is true that equity is now considered to some extent, it may not have the weight it deserves and it may, on occasion, be overlooked altogether. The danger in ignoring equity in theory is that it may be ignored in practice too, and we may find ourselves adopting policies that would be rejected if their political implications were taken into account.

In treating equity as a criterion for economic policy, our concern is not so much with inequity as with the absence or attenuation of equity. Inequity occurs when a well established standard is violated. Equity is attenuated when society ceases to have clear rules as to who has the right to what. There is inequity when a man whose house is expropriated because the land is needed for a new road is inadequately compensated and denied access to a legal means of pressing his claim to better treatment. There is an absence of equity when, as it were, a man and his neighbours do not know whether a particular house belongs to him, or when rights of ownership are so ill-defined that no one can say what a house is worth. Equity in the housing market would be attenuated in this sense if disputes between landlord and tenant could only be resolved by appeal to a board of overseers instructed to judge between them according to the needs of the individuals concerned, a procedure in which the disposition of houses would, in all probability, come to depend upon the wealth, religion, social class or political persuasion of the parties to a dispute. The concept of equity in the housing market pertains less to the content of rights than to their specification, for the rights and obligations of tenants can be defined in any of a variety of ways without equity being attenuated. Nor need a change in tenants' rights lead to an attenuation of equity if the new rules are well-defined and reasonably permanent – not expected to change substantially back and forth with every change of government or shift of political power.

The emphasis on equity is especially important in the light of the continued growth of government expenditure and government activity in the economy throughout this century. The larger the role of government, the more must it interact with the private sector, and the more frequently do occasions arise where the government cannot avoid determining who shall prosper and who shall not, as a natural and inevitable consequence of decisions it has to make. The growth of government is to some extent unavoidable, for it is a reflection of the increasing complexity of our technology, of the demand for the redistribution of income and of a commitment by society as a whole that no one is to become desperately poor. But as government grows and as equity is correspondingly attenuated, it becomes increasingly important that programmes not absolutely essential on other grounds are rejected when their impact on equity is adverse.

Feasibility must be the first consideration. In assessing economic policy, one wants to know the effect of each option upon the role of government in the assignment of income. Does a policy cause the incomes of the different groups in society to become more dependent upon negotiations with other groups than upon productive efforts on their own behalf? Does it create a situation where the personality, beliefs, ethnic loyalties or regional origins of the men in office have more effect upon the incomes of citizens than would otherwise be the case? Or does it make the system of equity more feasible by clarifying the rules under which each person or group may act in its own interest? Of course, equity is not an all-or-nothing proposition, and some attenuation of the system of equity may be a fair price to pay for a substantial increase in the size of the national income or a major reduction in inequality. Society can and does live with a degree of feasibility (defined, it will be recalled, as the percentage of a typical man's income determined prior to and independently of the political process) that is less than 100 per cent. The most that can be expected from a particular reform is a marginal increase in the degree of feasibility or a strengthening of the system of equity in its effect upon some industry or social class. Attenuation, on the other hand, is simply a movement on the continuum from perfect equity, where the assignment of income is entirely and completely independent of all political influence, towards the opposite pole, where income is assigned in the legislature in the manner discussed in Chapter 2.

Acceptability, though subordinate, is also important. No system of equity, however feasible in itself, will serve as a foundation for democratic government unless citizens are prepared to accept its rules, for the majority can vote to change the rules at any time. The greater part of the defence of capitalism is precisely the knowlege that capitalism is feasible as a system of equity, and that it is, for all practical purposes, the only feasible system we know. The defence may none the less be insufficient in the presence of widespread poverty or great disparities of wealth. Capitalism is rendered more acceptable, and changes in society that might greatly attenuate the system of equity are forestalled by transfers of income from rich to poor through progressive income tax or other redistributive programmes. One of the trade-offs in the formation of economic policy is between feasibility and acceptability. Redistributive policies which might attenuate equity to some extent may be necessary to induce the disadvantaged members of the community to accept the system at all.

The object of this chapter is to show how equity interacts with efficiency and equality in the choice of economic policy. As we shall examine several types of economic policy, the discussion must be brief, just enough to show in each case how equity is relevant to the problem at hand. In some cases, I try to show how considerations of equity must be introduced to make sense of what we do. In others, I try to show how our failure to take equity seriously has led to policies detrimental to the continuance of democratic government. The discussion is organized under the headings of equity, equality and efficiency, according to the criterion that appears to predominate, but the emphasis is always on relations among the three.

POLICIES PRIMARILY AFFECTING EQUITY

Equity in capitalist countries is supported by the comprehensive tax base and by anti-trust policy. There have been proposals to foster social harmony by participation of workers and businessmen in decision-making in the firm and in the nation. There have been proposals to reinforce property rights and restrict the growth of government by imposing constitutional limits on tax rates so that approval of substantially more than half the electorate is required for tax rates to be increased. We shall consider these matters in turn.

The Comprehensive Tax Base

It is an ideal of tax reform that the multiplicity of taxes in society — income taxes, excise taxes, property taxes, corporation taxes and so on — be replaced by a single tax with a uniform base which is the same for everyone. The rate of tax may be higher for the rich than for the poor, but the base on which the rate is assessed is invariant. The leading candidate for the comprehensive tax base is income defined as the sum of '(1) the market value of the rights exercised in the consumption and (2) the change in the value of the store of property rights between the beginning and the end of the period in question.'[3] This definition is reflected more or less closely in the income tax codes of most Western countries, and there are attempts from time to time to move the whole tax structure closer to the ideal by broadening and refining the definition of income and eliminating other taxes as, for instance, was proposed by the Carter Commission in Canada.[4] Among tax lawyers and economists, there are differences of opinion as to what the base should be, a majority favouring income as defined above, but a substantial and growing minority favouring consumption alone. We are not here concerned with alternative definitions of the tax base. We are concerned with the principle that simplicity itself is a virtue — that a single tax with a well-defined base is preferable to a tax system with many different kinds of taxes and numerous exceptions and qualifications to the rules.

Why might such a principle be attractive? It is not merely an application of utilitarianism to public finance, for a utilitarian criterion would allow people with the same income to be taxed at different rates according to the effects of the tax on the supply of labour and consumption of different commodities; the more a man's labour supply is reduced by a given rate of tax, the greater is the social cost of the tax, and the lower the rate of tax on that man ought to be.[5] The reason for wanting a comprehensive tax base − a reason so simple it is hardly ever expressed in so many words − is to keep people from fighting over the apportionment among citizens of the cost of public services; for a political decision as to how much each person must pay for public services has many of the features and many of the consequences of simple political assignment of income discussed in Chapter 2. The ideal of the comprehensive tax base is an assignment of taxes so obviously fair and appropriate that all conflict over payment for the services of government would be eliminated. Allow farmers to pay different taxes than plumbers, homeowners to pay different taxes than tenants, easterners to pay different taxes than westerners − and we are in danger of losing the consensus on which democratic government depends.[6]

Though the ideal of the comprehensive tax base has always been recognized to some extent in the formation of tax systems in democratic societies, it has never been the only consideration. The cost of collection is relevant, and the inequity from not having a comprehensive tax base must be balanced against the frequently greater inequity resulting from tax evasion. There is also a need to distinguish between services provided by the public sector to particular individuals and public goods that cannot benefit one man without benefiting everyone else as well; a train ride on the state railway is an example of the former and the army is the standard example of the latter. As a rule, the first type of service is financed by pricing, more or less as is done in the private sector, and it is only to the financing of the latter type that our discussion of the comprehensive tax base applies. The issue is complicated by the fact that many of the services provided by the public sector have characteristics of both 'private' and 'public' goods.

There are proposals in the literature of public finance for new tax systems that would make the comprehensive tax base unnecessary. The present tax structure, composed of the personal income tax, the corporation income tax, sales taxes, tariffs, and so on, would be replaced by a system in which each man is taxed according to his marginal valuation of the services of public goods. The centerpiece of all such proposals is a bidding scheme in which each taxpayer reveals his marginal valuations in the process of indicating how much of each type of service he wants the public sector to supply. As yet the bidding schemes themselves seem unworkable in practice, and there is no evidence that voters would be inclined to redefine and extend property rights as these proposals require.[7] At a minimum, the cost of redistribution would have to be apportioned among citizens on some principle other than taxation according to the benefit of public expenditure. The political advantages of a comprehensive tax base remain as long as not all tax can be apportioned among citizens according to the value of the services they receive.

Anti-trust

Despite the prohibition of monopolistic practices in the common law, and almost 100 years after the passage of the Sherman Anti-Trust Act in the United States, there remains a deep cleavage among students of anti-trust in their interpretations of what the law is supposed to do. The terminology by which lawyers and economists discuss anti-trust does not quite correspond to the terminology in this book, but we can capture some of the spirit of the controversy by attributing to one side the view that business practices should be assessed in the law according to a criterion of efficiency alone, and to the other side the view that anti-trust policy should be guided by considerations of efficiency and equity together.

Views conflict particularly over the question of whether an industry should be allowed to concentrate when the larger firms are more efficient in the sense that output can be produced at a lower price. Is anything lost if an industry that once contained 50 firms evolves, through merger or failure of less efficient firms, until there are only three firms left, and if competition among the remaining three is still vigorous enough that prices are lower than they would have been had the number of firms not declined? Those who believe that efficiency is the only appropriate criterion for anti-trust policy would say that nothing is lost in the decline in the number of firms; they would emphasize that the law seeks to protect 'competition not competitors', and that the welfare of the consumer, the only relevant consideration, is not adversely affected as long as prices are not raised over and above what would have occurred if the number of firms in the industry had remained the same.[8]

Those concerned with equity and efficiency together have a more difficult case to make because there is no clear principle as to how the criteria are to be balanced one against the other. But if equity is relevant and important, it cannot be excluded on that ground alone, for society makes many trade-offs among criteria in circumstances where there is no well defined higher criterion in which the lower criteria may be subsumed. What we are calling the equity criterion is implicit in the following statement by Chief Justice Peckham from a judgement of the US Supreme Court in 1897. 'Business combinations', he said,

> . . . may even temporarily, or perhaps permanently, reduce the price of the article traded in or manufactured, by reducing the expense inseparable from the running of many different companies for the same purpose. Trade or commerce under those circumstances may nevertheless be badly and unfortunately restrained by driving out of business the small dealers and worthy men whose lives have been spent therein and who might be unable to readjust themselves to their altered surroundings. Mere reduction in the price of the commodity dealt in might be dearly paid for by the ruin of such a class.[9]

The rationale for protecting 'small dealers and worthy men' at the expense of the consumer has been stated by Kaysen and Turner in language closely related to the central concerns of this book. They identify four aims of anti-trust policy: desirable economic results, promoting competitive processes, insuring fair conduct and limiting big business. They justify the last objective as follows:

> The goal of a 'proper' distribution of power between large and small business is rationalized in terms of certain Jeffersonian symbols of wide political appeal and great persistence in American life: business units are politically irresponsible, and therefore large powerful business units are dangerous. The political and social power of the independent proprietor is the foundation of democracy; therefore his power as against that of the corporate bureaucrat must be maintained or re-established. The power of absentee ownership and management in relation to the local community and local and state governments must be diminished, lest the failure of state and local control provoke an increase in federal intervention in both business and local community life, and a corresponding increase in federal power. These doctrines, often in inchoate form, undoubtedly provide an important emotional substratum on which political support for anti-trust policy of some kind rests.[10]

A concern for equity leads to the view that monopoly *per se* is dangerous even if large firms charge lower prices than small firms would have done. It leads to the view that 'structure' is important over and above the 'performance' of the industry. It leads to the view that society should seek ways of breaking up large firms even without evidence of specific behaviour against the public interest, by making size or monopoly position alone grounds for dissolution or, more gently, by instituting a progressive corporation income tax to induce large firms to break up voluntarily unless the advantages of scale outweigh the tax advantages of being small.[11]

The policy implications of the efficiency-and-equity criterion are made doubly complex by the ever-present risk that action by government to preserve the appearance of competition will lead to a situation where the maintenance of the existing industrial structure and the prosperity of a great many small firms become directly dependent on the goodwill or favour of the government, precisely as has happened to many firms in the regulated sector of the economy. Once efficiency is abandoned as the sole criterion for public supervision of business practice, we run the risk of inefficient firms becoming clients of the state and, as there is no fixed rule as to how much inefficiency is the proper price to pay for a given improvement in industrial structure (whether the reduction of the number of firms from 50 to three is better or worse from a social point of view than a 1 per cent increase in the price of the output), we may find that government action in support of competition leads precisely to the problems of faction that the policy is designed to avoid. Perfect competition if feasible is a system of equity. An industrial structure that looks like competition but is what it is because of deliberate government policy to make it so may lack the essential quality of equity, that the assignment of income to citizens is independent of decisions taken in the public sector.

If, as Marx asserted and many supporters of the capitalist system continue to fear, the natural tendency of completely unregulated capitalism is towards a world of monopolies, or if technical change, especially in computation and communication, is creating economies of scale so large as to generate monopolies in a great many industries – if either of these propositions is true, then some public sector activity is required to preserve the environment for capitalism, and the risk of firms becoming clients of the regulatory arm of the state must be borne, though the seriousness of the risk can be lessened by the judicious choice of regulatory or anti-trust policy. A progressive corporation income tax would seem to have many advantages in this context. There are, on the other hand, those who argue that the natural direction of capitalism is towards competition rather than monopoly, while the propensity of government regulation of business has on the whole been precisely the reverse. Recall the evidence in Chapter 5 that concentration by industry as measured by four-firm concentration ratios has not increased significantly in the United States in this century, and that the share of manufacturing output of the largest 100 firms has stabilized in the 1950s and 1960s after rising for many years. It is difficult to say whether this is due to the effectiveness of anti-trust or to the intrinsic vigour of competition.

Co-determination and the Corporate State

These forms of organization are treated together here because they have been advocated as remedies for the same disease of capitalism and they are, in my opinion, defective for the same reason.

Co-determination is a way of organizing a firm so that workers, managers and owners all participate in policy formation, usually by having representatives of all groups on the board of directors. It is a broad concept, extending all the way from the placing of a token worker on the board of directors to the complete ownership of the firm by the work-force as is alleged to occur in Yugoslavia. The corporate state is a state in which the governing body is composed of representatives not of geographical constituencies, but of the industrial classes: manufacturing workers, owners of firms, farmers, professors, lawyers and so on. There has never, to my knowledge, been a pure and complete corporate state — Italian fascism, though it used the name, was really quite different — but steps in that direction have been taken informally in Britain where leaders of trade unions and business associations have been regularly consulted on economic policy.

The common origin of co-determination and the corporate state is that they are both ways of dealing with the political consequences of the struggle between workers and owners over the assignment of the national income. The central idea is that, if you can bring workers and owners together, they will find a way of resolving their differences harmoniously without the strikes and political agitation endemic in a capitalist economy.

It is important in assessing these forms of economic organization to recognize that the struggle between workers and owners cannot occur in a perfectly competitive economy because all prices of goods, rents of factors of production and wages of labour are determined impersonally in the market. Conflict over assignment between workers and owners can occur only to the extent that actual capitalism deviates from the model through bilateral monopoly in the firm, industry or nation, or through lack of consensus as to who really owns the different factors of production. We discussed bilateral monopoly in Chapter 5. Recall how the market broke down when all bread producers and all cheese producers formed rival associations. The parties were no longer able to rely on the market to establish a trade of bread for cheese because the rivalries among bread producers and among cheese producers were eliminated. Precisely the same situation may arise between workers and owners. When all workers in the coal industry confront all mine owners together, the rivalry among workers seeking jobs and among owners seeking employees is eliminated and there is no economic principle by which wages can be set. In fact, it is because bilateral monopoly occurs much more frequently in labour markets than in goods markets that wage-setting, rather than price-setting, is the more prone to give rise to acrimony between the parties, to loss of output in the process of negotiation and to political influence in the assignment of income to citizens. There is no need for an equivalent of the Taft-Hartley Act in the goods market — no provision in law for a cooling-off period if tomato growers and tomato consumers cannot agree on a price — for it is taken as a matter of course that a price will, one way or another, get set each day. There is no counterpart in the goods market to the miners' strike in the United Kingdom in 1974 where a conflict over allocation led to a change in government in a political crisis which, at the time, seemed so serious that people began to wonder whether democratic government would not in the end be destroyed through its failure to reconcile the claims of the different social classes.

Neither co-determination nor corporatism is likely to be helpful in this context. Conflict over the setting of wages is a manifestation of the attenuation of the capitalistic system of equity through bilateral monopoly in the market for labour. There would be much to be said for co-determination or corporatism if they provided an alternative. My objection to these forms of economic and political organization is that they do no such thing. They do not provide new principles for the apportionment of the national income; they eliminate whatever guidance the competitive market might supply. A board of directors composed, let us say, of equal numbers of workers and owners has no principle whatsoever to guide it in dividing the earnings of the firm between workers and owners. Depending on who gets the upper hand, the wages of labour can be reduced to the level at which workers seek alternative employment — a very low level in a society where worker participation in the direction of the firm gives each firm an incentive not to accept extra workers from outside the firm — or raised to the point where all remuneration to the so-called owners is eliminated. In these circumstances, characterized not by inequity but by the complete absence of equity, the assignment of incomes is more and more determined by the state because, contrary to expectations when co-determination is introduced, it becomes literally impossible to assign income in any other way.

Precisely the same problem arises on a national scale when the overall assignment of the national income is determined by bargaining between representatives of the trade union congress and the national employers' association. This is bilateral monopoly on the widest possible scale, and there is no more reason to suppose that an amicable solution will emerge at this level than there is when bilateral monopoly occurs in wage-setting for an industry or a firm. Corporatism would, no doubt, supply numerous occasions for creative statesmanship on the part of national leaders. We would see crises averted by heroic compromises. We would experience an escalation of threats and ever-more politicized communities of workers and owners, with serious and costly confrontations from time to time as negotiation breaks down. And we would come to forget that the crises, negotiations and statesmanship would be largely unnecessary if the market had been preserved. Co-determination and corporatism are not cures for a disease of capitalism; they are extreme, virulent and self-inflicted forms of that very disease.

Such industrial strife as we have experienced in North America has not been so costly or so divisive as to interfere with long-term economic growth or the continuance of democratic institutions. There is much to be said for continuing to muddle through as we have in the past, or, if we innovate at all, to try to reduce the extent of bilateral monopoly in the economy by reducing the authority of unions over their membership, lessening the cohesiveness of businesses in the same industry through vigorous anti-trust policy, and making strikes more costly to all parties involved. Labour relations might be improved if governments, instead of trying to negotiate settlements, took a hostile and vindictive attitude to union and management together whenever the public was adversely affected by a strike. Perhaps unions and firms might both be fined for conspiracy to restrict trade, regardless of which party actually initiated the work stoppage.

Constitutionalism

By constitutionalism, I refer to the view that a large part of the rules of society should be included in a constitution that can be amended only by the agreement of substantially more than a bare majority of the voters.[12] The way to stop majorities from abusing the power of the vote to dispose of minorities in the manner described in Chapter 2 is to limit voting so that this is no longer possible. The constitutional route is increasingly advocated by those who are alarmed at the growth of government in recent decades and see no prospect of containing or reversing the trend unless constitutional limits on taxation and expenditure are imposed. The ideal would be to replace majority rule with unanimity, such as arises automatically in exchanges in a free market. If I have bread and you have cheese, a voluntary agreement between us to exchange some of my bread for some of your cheese is unanimous if we two constitute the whole of society, and it preserves some of the character of unanimity when there are more than two people because the rest of the population preserves what it had before our agreement was struck. Voting is different. If you, I and a third party constitute a community with unlimited majority rule, you and I can combine to take what we please from the third party. The problem of faction in Chapter 2 can be looked upon as arising because the essential unanimity required for commercial transactions does not extend to transactions in the political realm. The proposed solution is to make unanimity a requirement in politics as well.

Though unanimity is the ideal, it is not advocated in practice because of bargaining anomalies that would result. If unanimity is required for the passage of a new law, it becomes profitable for any man to hold the community to ransom by threatening to vote against the law, even when he personally stands to gain from having it passed. Imagine a community of 15 people, each with an income of $10 initially, and suppose the effect of a proposed law would be to raise every man's income to $11. Each man has an incentive to vote for the law, but Mr 1 may announce that he will vote against it unless given a premium of, say $2.80 ($0.20 from each of the remaining voters) over and above the $1 he would get automatically. Since each voter is in a position to make such a threat, it becomes difficult to pass laws at all, and society becomes completely rigid or less prosperous than it might otherwise be. It is in order to avoid this outcome, and to draw a balance between the difficulties of majority rule and the costs of change under a unanimity rule, that people who favour unanimity as an ideal are usually inclined to advocate a two-thirds or three-quarters rule instead.

Specifically, the new constitutionalism is reflected in a number of proposed amendments, some adopted and some not, to the constitutions of certain states of the United States. The amendments differ in detail from state to state, but they always require something more than a simple majority of the legislature — perhaps a referendum or a two-thirds majority — for tax rates to be increased. California's Proposition 13 also reduced property taxes by over 50 per cent and included a sufficiently small inflation adjustment that the real value of taxes can be expected to decline from year to year if inflation continues at its present rate.

It might be supposed that a concern for equity would lead one to favour a constitutional remedy for the excesses of government spending. Equity is, after all, very much like a constitution for the economy. A system of equity is a set of rules of assignment of income that the legislature agrees to respect. To embed the rules in a constitution would seem to reinforce their acceptance and to make it less likely that they will be violated.

A written constitution can be especially helpful in resolving what has come to be known as the assurance paradox.[13] There are rules that I am entirely willing to follow, even when I have the power to do otherwise, if and only if I am confident that others will follow the rules as well. When my party is in office, I will not disenfranchise you or take away your livelihood as long as I can be confident that my right to vote and my livelihood will be guaranteed when my party loses at the polls and your party takes power instead. A constitutional guarantee of the right to vote removes, or at least alleviates, each man's fear that he will be disenfranchised by his opponents. It does so directly, by requiring a larger proportion of the population to disenfranchise a person through a constitutional amendment than would be required in an ordinary vote, and it does so indirectly, by removing or weakening the principal incentive of a government in power for disenfranchising its opponents.

But the use of a constitution to strengthen rules that no majority would violate, except in fear, should be distinguished from its use to oppose policies a permanent majority may wish to adopt. A majority may, for instance, wish to raise taxes to increase social security or for assistance to the poor. A provision of the constitution requiring a two-thirds majority to raise tax rates is not like a provision forbidding a government to disenfranchise its opponents, for everyone is content as long as no one is disenfranchised, while the will of the majority may be blocked by the will of a minority when approval of two-thirds of the voters is required to increase tax rates. There is no assurance that what the constitution forbids at any given time is necessary as a prerequisite to democracy. If, as we have argued in the last chapter, a degree of redistribution of income strengthens the system of equity in capitalism by making capitalism more acceptable to the less prosperous members of the community, then a constitutional limit on taxation could attenuate the system of equity to some extent by provoking the majority to acts less compatible with democratic government than the tax increase would have been.

No constitution can stop a determined majority from getting what it wants. A majority may back down if its immediate interests seem in conflict with a long-term gain. But if, after all the pros and cons are weighed, it is decided that a law or policy is in the interest of the majority, and if the matter is important, then the constitution will be changed or circumvented by packing the Supreme Court, as Roosevelt threatened to do, with judges who can be counted upon to 'understand the public interest'.

It is frequently alleged by advocates of constitutional limits on taxation that their proposal *is* in accordance with the will of the great majority of voters, but that the voters' desire for lower taxes and less public expenditure is systematically frustrated by their elected representatives. Elected representatives become the captives of civil servants seeking to expand their sphere of influence, or the elected representatives' need for campaign funds and their limited access to information leads them to favour special, concentrated interests, seeking higher spending, over the more general interest in keeping taxes low. Two men who would each gain $13 from a given policy may have a greater incentive to lobby the legislature than 13 men, each of whom would lose $2 if the policy were adopted; and, politics being what it is, the two are likely to get their way.

While not denying that the will of the majority can, on occasion, be distorted in the electoral process, I find it difficult to believe that this phenomenon can account for the historical rise in public spending. The majority can, after all, elect representatives who promise to reduce public spending, and it can refuse to re-elect them if the cost of increased taxes is considered to exceed the benefit of what the taxes are used to buy. The 13 can always outvote the two, and only deception on the part of the latter will prevent the former from doing so. Note that the example in the paragraph above is the exact opposite of the example we considered in Chapter 2. There the problem was to keep the majority from expropriating the minority; now the peculiarities of the electoral process have enabled the minority to expropriate the majority. I believe that the problem was correctly posed in the first instance, and that, if any minority is to get the upper hand, it will be the minority of the rich with the means to buy influence and to lobby elected representatives of the voters, a minority with an interest in low taxes and correspondingly reduced public services. A majority may, of course, be mistaken in its assessment of its interests. To say that its will is systematically thwarted in the election process is to invoke a rhetoric of conspiracy, a dangerous rhetoric that breeds conspiracy in self-defence and tends to weaken the trust on which democracy depends. The rhetoric of constitutional limits on taxation and expenditure is frequently about exorbitant tax rates, irresponsible politicians and bureaucrats gouging taxpayers – with strong overtones of an adversary relation between the citizen and the government. The simple fact may .be that the public sector has grown because the majority wanted it so. One does, however, get the impression that there is a change of mood in North America, a feeling that public expenditure has grown enough and ought to be stabilized or reduced. It is not clear why departure from simple majority rule would be warranted in these circumstances.

There is also a technical problem in trying to embed the rules of the economy in a constitution. Any method of decision-making, other than majority rule itself, requires the positive identification of the *status quo*. A two-thirds rule, a three-quarters rule or a unanimity rule all require that, when an issue comes up for resolution, it is possible to say with certainty what the law is and what constitutes a change in the law. All issues can be thought of as located on a continuum: at one pole are those issues, like whether a person can be imprisoned because the police chief wants to take away his house, where the *status quo* is as exact as human rules can be. At the other pole are issues, like whether Mr X or Mr Y shall become president (neither being an incumbent), where no *status quo* can be identified. We most certainly do not use majority rule in deciding whether the police chief can have his way, but we have no alternative to majority rule in electing a president because any other rule would either give one man an unfair advantage or create the possibility of the country's not being able to elect a president at all.

A great many issues lie in a grey area where there is some sense of *status quo* but room for disagreement as to just what the *status quo* implies. Who has the right to the use of a river? Is busing of schoolchildren mandatory in a particular city? When can the prime minister order the violation of property rights in a national emergency? What constitutes a violation of the rights of privacy? How much tax do I owe? Legislators are continually having to enact new laws because new conditions, new technology or new social standards give rise to problems not anticipated when the existing laws were passed. Though a constitutional limit on taxation or public expenditure might be better specified than some other types of rules, it would not be entirely free from ambiguity and the *status quo* would not be beyond dispute. A national constitutional limit on taxation or public expenditure would require a specification of what constitutes tax and expenditure, and an exemption for emergencies to avoid paralysing the country in the event of war. Judicial interpretation — especially in circumstances where the constitution appears to thwart the will of a determined majority — could nullify the limitation or be quite capricious in its implications. The more that is prohibited under a constitution, the greater the influence of the judiciary on policy, and the greater the temptation upon the legislators to allow political considerations to determine who the judges will be.

We can, therefore, identify several reasons why it may be harmful or self-defeating to use the constitutional amendment to stop growth of government expenditure and reduce the influence of government on the economy. There is, first, a real possibility that a constitutional limitation on taxation or public spending would be either redundant (in the event that voters do not want to increase public spending and ordinary legislation reflects the will of the majority) or ineffective (because a majority that does want to increase public spending succeeds one way or another in having public spending increased). There is a danger of redirecting discussion of economic policy from the relatively straightforward issue of what we wish to buy through the public sector and how we wish to pay for it to sophistical arguments about when a tax is a tax and when an expenditure is an expenditure. Economic policy could be distorted toward devious and costly expedients because the best way to achieve a given objective is blocked to a majority not large enough to revise the constitution. A constitutional limitation on taxation alone could easily lead to inflation, as the creation of new money becomes the only way to finance extra public expenditure. There is the danger that a society that denies itself the right to levy taxes and to change some rules of property by majority voting will redirect political activity to the constitution. Politicians will become increasingly careful to appoint judges whose interpretation of the law can be expected to favor the right political party or social class. This is, of course, a difficulty with any constitution; but the difficulty, which is manageable as long as the constitution is limited to simple rules the vast majority of citizens are inclined to accept, becomes a threat to the constitution with the growth of the number, complexity, ambiguity and unpopularity of the privileged rules. There is the risk, to those who use the constitution to limit taxation or public expenditure, of the constitution becoming more flexible and of other, less attractive sorts of economic policy becoming entrenched. Today tax limitation becomes a privileged item of policy requiring more than half of the voters to overturn. Tomorrow it may be rent control, or the size of the old age pension, or socialized medicine. We could end up with a hodge-podge of rules with different constitutional status depending on nothing more than the peculiarities of voting history. There is the possibility of the constitution losing the respect it now enjoys as it becomes the object of, rather than the framework for, party politics. To serve its primary purpose of resolving the assurance paradox, the constitution must be thought of as permanent. Too great a willingness to amend the constitution could lead to a situation where no constitional provision — not even civil rights — is respected above ordinary laws. And, finally, there is a risk of the constitution being used by an interested minority to prevent changes that would enhance the acceptability of capitalism as a system of equity. A constitution that prevented the majority from altering the rights of property would, at various times, have rendered unconstitutional child labour laws (economic freedom is violated if a willing employer and a willing child cannot negotiate a labour contract), the income tax, and the prohibition of slavery. A majority that finds itself blocked by the constitution may, in desperation, violate the constitution or take steps more damaging to democratic government than what the constitution actually forbids.

The unanimity rule is fine if you approve of the laws as they are. It can be tyrannous if more than half the population wants to change them. It can turn into a minority rule if a political party succeeds in packing the Supreme Court with judges whose interpretation of the law differs from what the majority believes the law to be. There may ultimately be no substitute for a population that understands where its true, long-term interests lie and is prepared to leave enough of the capitalist system intact as is necessary as a prerequisite to democracy.

POLICIES PRIMARILY AFFECTING EQUALITY

Transfer to Persons

Gradually, over the last 100 years, most countries in Western Europe and America have developed elaborate systems of transfer payments to persons, to firms, and among jurisdictions. Old age pensions and transfers to the poor have come to account for virtually all of the income of people in the lowest quintile of the income distribution in the United States.[14] Transfers from the federal government constitute a not inconsiderable part of the revenue of state or provincial governments, and transfers from the state or provincial governments constitute a large part of the revenue of local governments. Farmers receive transfers in the form of agricultural price supports. Tariffs and import quotas may be looked upon as transfers among domestic industries. The tax code contains numerous exemptions that acquire an ever-greater importance as marginal tax rates increase. It is, of course, a matter of definition and convention whether items in the tax code such as mortgage deductability and accelerated depreciation should be looked upon as transfers. What is important is that these items affect the incomes of different taxpayers and the profitability of firms just as agricultural price supports affect the incomes of farmers and social security affects the welfare of the old, and that each of these programmes is supported politically by the favoured group.

So prevalent have transfers become that economists have begun to speak of a 'transfer society', a 'grants economy', a 'rent-seeking' society, or more colourfully, an 'economy of love and fear', the idea being that love and fear are the two principal motives for the granting of transfers and that they somehow interact to generate an equilibrium set of transfers in a manner analogous to the way supply and demand interact in the market to generate an equilibrium set of prices.[15] Most economists are uneasy about the transfer society. They see it as wasteful and inefficient, for the possibility of the government supplying hand-outs diverts energy from making things people need to political activity for directing hand-outs to one's own group.[16] There may also be pronounced effects upon the system of equity. Our example in Chapter 2 was, after all, an extreme instance of a transfer society, a society where a majority of voters may give or withhold income at will and where the whole of one's income is dependent on the goodwill of one's fellow citizens. The growth of transfers as a percentage of the national income attenuates equity by degrees, pushing the economy toward ever-greater political assignment of income.

But it is, in my opinion, a mistake to suppose that all transfers are alike in their effects upon the system of equity. In particular, there is a place in the analysis of the effects of transfers for the distinction discussed in Chapter 3 between redistribution and reassignment of income. A redistributive transfer is a systematic transfer of income from all rich people to all poor people undertaken in such a way that no one changes rank on the scale of rich and poor. A reassignment is a grant to whatever person or group the legislature chooses to favour at the moment regardless of whether the favoured group is rich or poor. The distinction is important because, within limits, redistribution favours capitalism as a system of equity by making it more acceptable, while reassignment is almost invariably corrosive.

From our discussion of the acceptability of capitalism in the last chapter, we can identify three reasons why redistributive transfers can support democratic government. The first is that redistribution has a natural equilibrium and stopping place. As more and more income is transferred from rich to poor, the marginal tax rates required to effect the transfer have to rise and total output is diminished until a point is reached where the median voter has more to lose from the adverse effect on total output than he has to gain from his share of the redistributed income. Once that point is reached, a majority of voters begins to oppose further redistribution and the process stops. There is no comparable equilibrium in reassignment. Let it be known that reassignment is possible, and every regional, ethnic or industrial interest group is at once at war with every other group over the division of the spoils; every common interest, every bond among subgroups of citizens, becomes a nucleus around which people may coalesce in the scramble for private access to public funds.

The second reason has to do with allegiance of the poor. Though differences in wealth and status are not greater under capitalism than what has been observed under other forms of economic organization, the poor, if their lot is bad enough, may have an incentive to try their luck with a different form of economic organization in the hope that their personal income and status may rise, though the national income as a whole may not. Redistribution makes this less likely, for the better off one is, the less one can expect to gain from a given reorganization. I may be content with the rules of capitalism, including the rules of inheritance under which I may start life at a considerable disadvantage by comparison with my contemporaries, if I can be assured of a minimum standard of living in any given year. It may, therefore, be in the interest of those who place special importance on the continuance of capitalism and democracy to push for a redistribution of income even beyond what the median voter would support if the balance between his share of the loss of total output and his gain from the redistribution were the only consideration.

The third reason why redistribution makes capitalism more acceptable has to do with the intrinsic uncertainty of the capitalist system. No one, however well off he may be this year, can be sure that his good fortune will continue. The loss of one's job, an unlucky speculation, or a change in the demand for one's product can turn a rich man into a poor man overnight. I will bear these risks with greater equanimity if I know there is a floor on the amount I stand to lose and if I, like any poor man, am guaranteed a minimal standard of living. A man whose income is high enough that he can expect to pay more in taxes to support redistribution than he is likely to receive over his life may none the less favour redistribution for this reason.

Though a sharp line cannot always be drawn between redistribution and reassignment of income, and most transfer programmes have some of the character of both general types, it is usually possible to say where, for all practical purposes, a particular programme belongs. The old age pension, socialized medicine, welfare, the family allowance and food stamps are primarily redistributive, while the transfer elements in farm price supports, tariffs and the industrial subsidies are primarily reassignments, for there is no presumption that the beneficiaries of the latter programmes are poor.[17]

There may, of course, be an element of reassignment in transfers to the poor. Some poor people may benefit at the expense of others or be eligible for special privileges not available to poor people generally. This occurs when welfare recipients are paid different amounts in different parts of the country, when members of groups specially designated as disadvantaged are given priority in admission to educational institutions, or when social services are denied to poor people not members of specially designated groups. Poor men are not all brothers. There is as much scope for social conflict among groups of poor people vying for grants as there is among any other set of groups in an overall reassignment of income.

It is in this context, I think, that the enthusiasm among professional economists for the negative income tax is to be understood. In theory, the negative income tax is the perfect redistribution with no element of reassignment at all. No group of poor people is privileged above any other. No civil servant need judge who deserves assistance and who does not, except in so far as statements of pretax income need to be verified for the poor as for everyone else.

Socialization of Goods and Services

Socialization is defined for the purpose of this book as the removal of a good or service from the private sector where each man buys as much as he pleases with the money at his disposal, to the public sector where whatever amount of the good or service is produced is divided up equally among all citizens. This is the sense in which the term is used when one speaks of socialized medicine. To socialize a good or service is to make the right to consume one's share of it an aspect of citizenship. Under socialized medicine, I have a right to medical service just as I have a right to vote. Medical services are socialized in Canada and the United Kingdom. Higher education is almost entirely socialized in the United Kingdom where students are granted generous scholarships to attend university, and it is largely socialized in Canada and in the United States, though many of the best American universities are found in the private sector. Elementary and secondary education is the other way around – almost entirely socialized in the United States and Canada, but less so in Britain where a large portion of the upper class is educated in private schools.

Other things being equal, socialization will be favoured by the poor and opposed by the rich because there is a redistribution of income when socialization is financed from the revenue of progressive or proportional taxes. But rich and poor alike are inconvenienced by the fact that everyone must consume the same amount of a socialized commodity. If cars were socialized, we would all have to drive the same size of car. The man who would prefer to drive a smaller, cheaper car and spend the extra money on the theatre and the man who would prefer to drive a larger, more expensive car and economize elsewhere are both harmed by socialization of cars and would both prefer that the redistributive element in socialization be administered directly, as in a negative income tax. It is partly for this reason that cars are not socialized, and that socialization is usually limited to a few items for which tastes tend not to differ very much from one man to the next, or where there are believed to be advantages in having the item supplied by the government.[18]

Though the redistributive element in socialization may promote the acceptability of capitalism, there is a real risk of equity being attenuated in the manner of apportionment of the socialized commodity among citizens. A commodity can be assigned to citizens by allowing each to take as much as he pleases, by providing the same amount to each person, or by a process of selecting recipients and deciding how much each shall have in accordance with a more or less well-specified criterion. The right of each citizen under socialized medicine to visit a doctor whenever he pleases is in accordance with the first method of assignment; the provision of identical access for all children to elementary schools is in accordance with the second; and the assignment of a limited supply of public housing to a group selected from a larger number of deserving poor is in accordance with the third, though elements of all three pure types are usually present in any given programme.

Equity need not be attenuated if either of the first two methods is adopted, that is, if enough of the commodity is produced for everyone to have as much as he pleases or if the available supply is divided equally among citizens. Assignment can be troublesome if free and unlimited access to the socialized commodity is considered too costly and if strict equality of provision cannot be maintained. Once medical care is socialized, there may develop pressures to provide extra services to the politically influential. Especially competent doctors, paid the same regardless of whom they treat, will be inclined to choose patients from among their own class or who can be helpful to them. Legislators will vie with one another to have good hospitals in their constituencies. Concern for the poor, which serves as the rationale for the establishment of public health services, could lead, in the end, to a situation where the rich or well connected get the same disproportionate medical services as before without having to pay for it. It is the converse of one of the major defects of the conscript army; the rich or well connected avoid the draft, while the poor, who are taken into the army in any case, are inadequately paid for the risk and discomfort they bear. A similar problem arises in higher education; the inequity in the assignment of places in universities may be greater than that in assignment of medical care because the beneficiaries constitute a minority of the population and are concentrated in upper-class families.

The most extreme and pitiful case of the attenuation of equity that has come to my attention has to do with the assignment of a socialized commodity. It concerns a famine in Bengal in the autumn of 1974. The distribution of grain had, for some time, been undertaken by the public sector. It was widely reported in the press that, when there was not enough grain to go around, the government of India chose to feed people in the cities and to let landless labourers in the countryside starve, because mobs in the city could cause great unrest while the landless labourers in the countryside were too dispersed to be dangerous. It should be stressed that the government of India did not act inequitably in this case. Once it is decided to place the provision of a commodity in the public sector, there is no equitable means of apportioning the total supply among people if the commodity cannot be distributed equally.[19]

There is another way for equity to be attenuated in socialization. The provision of a commodity in the public sector allows the government no choice but to decide how much of the commodity to supply, and this, in turn, has a marked influence on the remuneration of producers. An example will make this clear. There is not much of a problem in setting a wage for doctors in the public sector (in the Ministry of Health or in the army) when the number employed is a small proportion of the total supply in the country as a whole. Doctors in the public sector are simply paid the going wage of doctors in the private sector. The Civil Service Commission might not think of itself as following the market, and might be concerned to set a fair or just wage for the doctors it employs, but that would make little difference to the outcome of the contract because the market would set the standard of what is fair and just. In effect, the supply curve of doctors to the public sector is flat and the wage is set accordingly.[20] This is no longer true when all doctors are employed and all medical services are provided in the public sector. (The important consideration is that fees are set in the public sector; the independence of doctors in the conduct of their practice is not relevant to the problem at hand.) The public sector is now confronted with a rising supply curve of medical services from which a price-quantity combination must somehow be chosen. The public sector has no option but to set fees for the medical profession, knowing that it is, at the time, deciding what the incomes of doctors shall be.

The problem is complicated by a quality dimension. No matter how many or how few doctors are employed in the public sector, the government has a certain latitude in setting the wage because the quality of doctors in the public service would respond to the wage rate. The Civil Service Commission would, of course, hire the best man for the money. A high wage would attract a first-class medical service; a lower wage would attract a less competent cadre of doctors, and the quality of medical service in the public sector would be correspondingly lower. This latitude need not be inequitable when only a few doctors are employed in the public sector because the public sector gets what it pays for, as long as it hires intelligently. Something of the connection between wage and quality remains when all doctors are employed in the public sector, because a low wage drives some very good doctors out of the country and a high wage induces good doctors to immigrate. However, the main impact of the quality dimension is to widen the range of discretion in the setting of public sector wages, for there are now two variables – quantity and quality – over which the public sector may discriminate.

It is difficult to predict, in this context, how doctors' wages will be set. On the one hand, the legislature, being the only employer of doctors, may exploit its power to the full by setting wages as low as would be in the interest of the general public exclusive of the medical profession. On the other hand, the medical profession may organize to bargain with the government as a unit, in which case socialization leads naturally to a sort of bilateral monopoly, with the government on one side and doctors on the other.

The larger the public sector, the greater is the proportion of civil servants and their dependents in the electorate, and the more difficult it is for the government to take a hard line. Eventually, a point will be reached where public sector employees – alone or in combination with other social classes, such as old age pensioners and widows with dependent children whose incomes are primarily derived from the public sector – come to constitute a majority of the population of voters. As long as workers in the private sector constitute a majority, there is a continual pressure to keep wages of public servants down to the minimum required to hire people to do the work, and to set welfare payments and old age pensions at a level deemed appropriate by the taxpayer. All this changes when civil servants and wards of the state constitute a majority. Then the question is not how much the payers want to pay but how much the recipients can take without killing the goose altogether.

The prospect of a high-tax coalition of civil servants and wards of the state coming to dominate the legislature is dangerous, not so much because of the high taxes *per se*, though the resulting loss of efficiency may be considerable, but because there appears to be no system of equity that would permit the different groups in the coalition to divide the spoils among themselves. There are clear principles governing the determination of wage rates of civil servants and amounts of transfers to the poor as long as the legislature is dominated by the interests of voters as taxpayers, consumers of public goods and donors of transfer payments. But when the high-tax coalition constitutes a majority, there remains no alternative to political assignment of income in deciding, for instance, between the claims of teachers and higher civil servants or between the claims of old age pensioners and civil engineers. A legislature dominated by the high-tax coalition is like the 15-man example in Chapter 2. The prospect of a high-tax coalition is another reason for conducting redistribution in such a way as to limit the number of employees in the public sector. Direct redistribution is better than socialization from this point of view, and the negative income tax is probably best of all, though its disincentive effects may be considerable.[21]

Income Preservation

There is another sort of economic policy, which is often confused with redistribution but is, in fact, quite different in its effects. Economic policy may be designed to compensate for the uncertainty of the market and to protect individuals and groups against sudden and unexpected losses owing to forces beyond their control. Unemployment insurance is the prime example. Agricultural price support can be looked upon as policy of this sort, in so far as it is not simply tribute paid by the community at large to a group that happens to be over-represented in the legislature or particularly single-minded in its concerns. Trade policy through the setting of tariffs and quotas has been interpreted as the attempt by a country to shield its citizens from the adverse consequences of fluctuations in world prices. These policies differ fundamentally from redistribution because the beneficiaries are not necessarily poor. With reasonable mobility of labour across industries, the main beneficiaries of tariffs have to be the owners of capital in protected industries, and the corresponding losers are owners of capital in the rest of the economy. Even unemployment insurance may turn out to accrue as much to high-income as to low-income families.[22]

Policies to protect people or groups against an adverse turn of fortune can be justified on insurance principles or by reference to a conservative welfare function in which a decline in one's accustomed standard of living is worse than a condition in which one's income has been low all along.[23] According to the latter justification, I am worse off if my income falls from 15 to 10 than I would be if it had always been 10, and society should take steps to help me out, restoring my income to something approaching 15, though society need not concern itself with someone whose income has been constant at 10 for a long time.

Neither justification is persuasive in my opinion. Though the insurance argument may be valid in itself, it is unlikely that the benefits from insurance supplied in this roundabout way would be commensurate with the economic, political and social cost of a systematic attempt by the government to compensate for the ups and downs of the market. This is, in part, because there is no simple and obvious way of determining an average around which incomes fluctuate. One cannot always say in practice whether the decline in my income from 15 to 10 is from normal to below normal or from above normal to normal. Thus, the acceptance of the principle that normal income will be preserved is an invitation to conflict among social classes, each claiming its income to be below the norm. Furthermore, compensation for fluctuations of the market differs from ordinary insurance in an important respect. In ordinary insurance, the insured person is required to pay a premium to cover the expected value of the loss against which he is insured plus his share of the expense of administration. Schemes to compensate for fluctuations of the market typically make good the loss but do not tax the beneficiaries when they are prosperous. In the long run, farm price supports subsidize farmers, unemployment insurance subsidizes types of work where the rate of unemployment is unusually high, and tariffs always subsidize the protected industries. There is a systematic subsidization of industries where income tends to be variable and a built-in incentive for people to take risks that would be imprudent if society did not share the consequences of an unfavourable outcome.

The other justification, that having to do with the alleged conservative social welfare function, runs directly counter to the usual argument for redistribution. Redistribution is the transfer of income from rich to poor. A conservative social welfare function may justify the transfer of income from poor to rich. Suppose my income is normally 15 but sometimes falls to 10. I am better off over my life than a man whose income is always 10, but any transfer to me to preserve my income at 15 has to be financed by taxes of which the man whose income is always 10 must pay his share. If I do so badly in any year that I become poor, then presumably I am entitled to benefit like any poor man from the system of redistribution in force at the time. It is difficult to justify extra benefit because I used to be rich. A policy of preserving normal income would seem to have adverse consequences on efficiency, equality and equity as well.

POLICIES TO PROMOTE EFFICIENCY

In a society at once capitalist and democratic, the private sector of the economy has two main tasks to perform. It must produce the goods and services we require, and it must assign incomes to citizens. The objective in the first task is efficiency – the maximization of the national income. Part of the objective in the second task is equity – the minimization of the influence of the legislature on the assignment of income. I shall try to show in this section that the attempt to provoke firms to produce or to invest in socially desirable ways, to be efficient in the broadest sense of the term, can frequently undermine the essential role of the private sector in the assignment of incomes. The trade-off between equity and efficiency is frequently unrecognized, and policy that seems reasonable when efficiency alone is taken into account may appear unattractive when its full implications are appreciated. In particular, I want to argue that direct government influence upon the behaviour and profitability of firms – through subsidization of desirable behaviour, price and wage control, encouragement of monopolization, or participation of public corporations in the private sector – can do more harm in undermining the system of equity than can be justified by whatever benefits are likely to accrue from an improvement in the overall performance of the economy.

Viewed, as it were, from a distance, the organization of the economy appears as a great co-operative effort between government and business to produce the goods and services we consume. Government sets the rules, supplies the public goods including the army, the police, roads, schools and basic research, takes responsibility for keeping down unemployment and the rate of inflation, regulates products and processes that might be dangerous to the individuals or to the environment, levies taxes to finance these activities, and so on through a long list we need not set out in detail. Firms specialize in goods and services they are best equipped by experience and endowment of resources to produce, so that each worker and every machine is used in the industry or task where it can make the greatest contribution to the total output.

Up close, we see an entirely different picture. The dominant themes are rivalry and greed. Workers compete for jobs and businesses compete for sales and investment opportunities in a jungle where the common interest is no part of anyone's objective and where all but the most aggressive and efficient firms succumb in the end to bankruptcy or to absorption by larger or shrewder rivals. It is the central proposition of economics referred to in the quotations at the heading of Chapter 3 that these pictures, seemingly so different, do really fit together; that from rivalry and greed emerges a composition of output, a division of labour and an assignment of income to citizens with at least some of the desirable qualities one would expect from co-operation.

But the driving force of capitalism is greed none the less, and any attempt by the government to affect the composition of output may have adverse and unexpected consequences unless this elementary fact is taken into account. The legislature or the civil service, mistaking the outcome for the means, may suppose that firms will willingly co-operate with government in holding down prices or investing in socially desirable undertakings. Firms do so only if it is profitable. On learning that profitability is directly dependent on decisions of the legislature or civil service, businessmen have an immediate incentive to try to influence those decisions. Resources are diverted from production to lobbying, and there is a corresponding loss of output which could be more costly than the initial externality public intervention was intended to rectify. More relevant to our main concern is the possibility that public influence upon profits of individual firms, upon wages of workers in those firms, and upon the prosperity of the regions where those firms are located will cease to be directed by the impersonal goal of economic efficiency and will be transformed into political assignment of incomes as in the simple model of Chapter 2.

To argue, as we shall, that industrial policy may have adverse consequences upon the system of equity is not to argue that all government interference with business is unwarranted or that all regulation is counter-productive. There is, in my opinion, an answerable efficiency argument for public provision of infrastructure (not only roads and communications, but research that private firms have no incentives to do for themselves), for the setting of standards of quality, for the regulation of new drugs or products to ensure that they are safe, especially where the danger is not so much to the user of the product as to the environment as a whole, and for the public ownership or regulation of natural monopoly. It is precisely because of the long and growing list of things the government must do if the economy is to remain reasonably efficient, and because any government intervention in the economy attenuates equity to some extent, that special care is required to ensure that intervention is avoided except where the advantages of intervention are considerable and obvious.

The specification of an exact line of demarcation between public and private sectors may be as important as the choice of activities within the public sector. A capitalist system of equity can be squared with a certain amount of public sector activity, but the line between public and private should be clearly drawn, with business kept as completely as possible on one side and government kept as completely as possible on the other. It may not make a great deal of difference to the system of equity how society deals with a natural monopoly like the provision of electricity, as long as the rules for the pricing of electricity are well established. Provision of electricity might be in the private sector and heavily regulated, or it might be in the public sector altogether. It would make a considerable difference if the government feels free to vary rates from region to region, industry to industry, or even firm to firm according to some criterion of social justice or the needs of the individuals concerned. Similarly, not all regulation of firms need affect equity adversely. Safety regulations, applying equally to all firms and sufficiently precise to require minimal discretion on the part of the civil service, need not increase the dependence of firms on government to any significant extent and may enhance the acceptability of the system of equity in force. Safety regulations drafted in such a way that no one knows how and against whom they might be applied can have a very different effect. Investment subsidies or public ownership of firms in industries primarily on the private side of the line between public and private sectors attenuate the capitalist system of equity by making the profitability of firms less dependent on their ability to satisfy demands for goods and services and more dependent on the outcome of negotiation with government.

The trade-off between equity and efficiency will be illustrated with reference to the attempt by the government of Canada to influence pricing and investment decisions of firms through subsidization of investment, regulation of prices, wages, output and investment, and public ownership of firms in industries primarily in the private sector of the economy. As the emphasis is on the unrecognized effects of public policy on the system of equity, we will avoid the question of whether policy is really efficient or not. We shall give the courtesy title of efficiency to a group of policies adopted for a variety of reasons and justified by reference to the public interest, regardless of what their actual effects may be.

The Subsidization of Investment

Many countries have established elaborate programmes of subsidies to influence the amount, industrial composition and allocation among regions of investment in the private sector. Canada gives grants for a great variety of purposes. Among the more important programmes are the Regional Development Incentives Act which subsidizes investment to 'increase or maintain employment in designated regions of Canada', the Enterprise Development Program which provides 'a wide-ranging program of assistance to small and medium size business' to 'assist firms undertaking relatively high risk innovative or adjustment projects that can be expected to yield attractive rates of return', the Defence Industry Productivity Program which provides 'financial assistance to industrial firms for selected projects', the Industrial Research Assistance Program which encourages 'applied research in Canadian industry', the Shipbuilding Industry Assistance Program which subsidizes 'shipbuilders engaged in building and conversion of ships', and the Federal Business Development Bank which extends loans to businesses 'which do not have other sources of financing available to them on reasonable terms'.[24]

These programmes are intended to grant money (or lend at concessional interest rates) to firms as compensation for socially useful behaviour which would be unprofitable in the absence of the subsidies or as compensation for the detrimental effects of other public policies at home or abroad. In some respects the programmes are like commercial transactions between government and business, in which the government pays firms for doing what the government wants done. They are not intended to be capricious or to empower civil servants to confer benefits at will on some firms rather than others.

But that is exactly what these programmes do, for their objectives are typically so vague and so amenable to wider or narrower interpretation that the civil servants charged with the responsibility of carrying out these programmes have no choice but to exercise judgement as to whether a subsidy is warranted or not. Who can really discriminate among investments that 'increase or maintain employment in designated regions', or have 'high risk ... with attractive rates of return', or represent 'applied research', or 'do not have other sources of financing . . . on reasonable terms'? It is significant that there is no recourse to law by a firm that feels it has been wrongly denied a subsidy or has been harmed by the granting of a subsidy to a competitor. Nor could one recommend a legal remedy, except as a means for demonstrating the arbitrariness in these programmes, because the criteria for the programmes are not precise enough for the courts to decide whether they apply in a particular case.

The Regional Development Incentives Act provides a striking example of a criterion that cannot be applied in an equitable manner. The Act authorizes the Department of Regional Economic Expansion to subsidize firms for investing in less-developed regions of Canada only in those cases where 'it is probable that the facility would [not] be established . . . without the provision of such an incentive'. What firm could ever prove that it would not undertake a particular investment without a subsidy? More to the point, on what grounds might one dispute a civil servant's judgement that a firm would (or would not) undertake a particular investment without a subsidy? In effect, the Act authorizes the Department of Regional Economic Expansion to do as it thinks best in granting subsidies for the purpose of promoting investment in less-developed regions of Canada.

Industrial subsidy programmes tend to undermine the basis of equity because the unavoidable lack of precision in the objectives of these programmes compels civil servants to exercise judgements within a wide latitude as to whether a subsidy is warranted or not. The profitability of a firm becomes less a matter of its dealings with the public, the workforce and other firms, than of its effectiveness in negotiating with the government. In these negotiations, the civil servants and politicians are expected to act like the forces of nature, immune and impervious to special pleading or to political pressure. Sometimes I suppose they do, but there must develop very considerable pressures to act otherwise. A member of Parliament of the ruling party whose seat may be in jeopardy in the coming election pleads for an incentive grant to a firm contemplating the opening of a new plant in his constituency. The firm might establish the plant without the subsidy, or it might establish another plant in an equally less-developed region of the country. Who can tell? When a member of Parliament pleads for an incentive grant for a firm in his constituency, it might be wise to pay close attention and to issue the grant if the case for doing so is not completely without foundation. In fact, it is customary for the issuing of very large subsidies to be subject to approval by the Cabinet. Subsidization of a selection of firms pushes the economy a step along the road from market assignment of income to political assignment, increasing the scope for patronage and attenuating the system of equity to some extent.

The problem is complicated by the tendency of subsidies to breed more subsidies. Subsidies to the East give rise to demands for subsidies to the West. Subsidies to one firm give rise to demands for subsidies to others. And the clamour for assistance creates the impression that the private sector cannot stand on its own feet and that the government must step in to guide the private sector if the public interest is to be served.

There is, at the same time, a general weakening of whatever consensus there may have been, especially on the part of the poor, to tolerate the distribution of income that emerges in the private sector of the economy. We can accept the distribution of income when it is the outcome of a process that, if not exactly fair or just, is at least blind in its determination of who shall prosper and who shall not, a process that rewards effort and skill to some extent, and would seem to be irreplaceable if our political institutions are to be preserved. The situation changes as subsidies become an important determinant of incomes and as we move closer to a system of political assignment. We see a man prospering not, so it seems, because of his talents, or his inheritance, or even by chance, but because his firm was subsidized at a critical moment in its development. We see another man whose firm goes bankrupt because he fails to persuade officials that the management of his firm is progressive enough or that the prospects for the sale of his product are bright enough. We are less likely to tolerate disparities in income among citizens if they are seen as originating as grants from the public purse than if they are seen as the outcome of the impersonal forces of the market.

Subsidy programmes which keep firms from bankruptcy or forestall unemployment among their workers have an additional effect of preserving the status of the owners indefinitely. Such programmes insulate property owners from the ups and downs of the market, socialize the risk-taking function of ownership, and lead, in the end, to the elimination of the role of private property in the economy and to a transfer of control bit by bit to the state.

Regulation of Prices, Wages, Output and Investment

Industrial subsidies represent the most blatant departure from equity, for their use empowers the government — indeed, obliges the government — to have a say in the determination of the income of each particular and identifiable region, town and, in some cases, person in the country. But subsidization is not the only, or even the most important, means for the government to affect the assignment of income. Regulation of prices and wages, such as has been undertaken in Canada and the United States for short periods of time and appeared at one time to be a permanent feature of the British economy, can have a more pervasive and almost equally pointed influence. Price and wage control undermines the standard of equity because someone must be entrusted to set prices and wages and because he, in turn, must be responsible to the legislature. It is the problem of equity under socialism all over again, with the price controller playing the role of planner, with the same ambiguities as to how the planner is to reconcile conflicting interests, and with the same potentiality for the emergence of faction in the incentive each group acquires to use what political influence it has to insure that the planner will be friendly.

The effects of price control depend very much on the length of time the price control is maintained. If price control is maintained for a short time and then removed, the controller can fix all prices rigidly or allow prices to rise at a uniform rate. Temporary price control is often alleged to be useful for reversing inflationary expectations, though it is a matter of considerable dispute whether it can really be effective in that way. The situation changes radically when price control is maintained for a long time. The option of letting all prices increase at the same rate is no longer open, because changes in world prices or in local scarcities require changes in domestic relative prices to keep the economy reasonably efficient and to avoid bankruptcy of firms for which input prices have risen more rapidly than prices in the economy as a whole. Now the price controller has to decide when changes in relative prices are warranted. In doing so, he cannot avoid deciding whether profits of textile firms are appropriate, whether professors should be paid more or less than civil servants, and so on. Nor can the price controller rely on the market for the information he requires, because in controlling prices he eliminates their role as indicators of where true scarcities lie.

Each man's income comes to depend more and more on the goodwill of the price controller as it becomes progressively more difficult to supply objective criteria for deciding what prices shall be. The accumulation of transactions in response to the controlled price creates conditions, such as those one experiences in a city where rent control has been in force for a long time, where a substantial fraction of the population would be greatly harmed if the price control were removed. In this context, it is unlikely that the price controller will retain his independence. Prices will instead be determined by the legislature or the civil service in circumstances where the strike threat, party allegiance or simple bribery come to have a progressively larger role to play.

Other types of regulation affect equity in other ways. Canada maintains a Foreign Investment Review Agency to 'assess whether there is or will be significant benefit to Canada in proposals by non-Canadians regarding acquisition of control of Canadian business enterprises or the establishment of new businesses in Canada'.[25] One can imagine how the fortunes of Canadian firms might be affected by public decisions as to which domestic firms are to be protected from foreign competition.

In Canada, federal and provincial governments have been active in sponsoring monopoly in agriculture. The export of wheat was centralized during the Great Depression. Restriction of supply of other commodities, traditionally administered by the provinces through their exclusive jurisdiction over intra-provincial trade, has been extended to the country as a whole by the Farm Products Marketing Agencies Act of 1972. There are now nationwide, federally administered monopolies in eggs and poultry, and provincial monopolies in a great variety of farm products, including grains, pigs, milk, beef, vegetables, chickens and tobacco. Publicly sponsored monopoly in agriculture is consistent with no system of equity, because each farmer's income comes to depend primarily on how high a price the government sets for his crop or how large a crop the government allows him to produce. The farmer, in these circumstances, becomes like one of the 15 men in the example in Chapter 2, whose income depends on whether he succeeds in becoming a member of a majority coalition in the legislature.

Public Ownership of Firms

The public sector may choose to administer an entire industry, and it may own firms in industries containing many private firms as well. The former usually occurs where there is believed to be a natural monopoly, in which case it may make little difference whether the industry is nationalized or regulated. The latter occurs for a variety of reasons. It may be considered in the public interest for the nation as a whole to have a voice in a particular industry, especially if most firms in the industry are foreign-owned. The government may acquire a firm to prevent bankruptcy in a region where the firm is the major employer, because the continuance of the firm is considered desirable for reasons of national defence, or because the firm is believed to be a source of technical change.

Both forms of public ownership can attenuate the system of equity, but ownership of an entire industry does so by requiring that wages in the industry be politically determined, as discussed above in connection with the medical profession, while ownership of firms in predominantly private industries does so by affecting the profitability of other firms. Public ownership of firms is not necessarily harmful to private competitors. Privately owned firms may do very well if the publicly owned firm turns out to be inefficient, if entry to the industry is restricted, and if prices are set to enable the publicly owned firm to show a profit.

On the other hand, a publicly owned firm can wreak havoc among its privately owned competitors if it uses profit in one sector to finance price-cutting in another, or if its deficits are covered by general revenue. In either case, the public firm has a direct impact upon the profitability of its rivals in the private sector, and creates an incentive on their part to use political means to influence its behaviour.

There are hundreds of firms in the public sector in Canada under provincial and federal jurisdication.[26] Perhaps the most extreme example of unconstrained acquisition by government of firms in industries predominantly in the private sector is the Canada Development Corporation. Established in 1971, its mandate is

> to develop and maintain strong Canadian controlled and managed corporations in the private sector of the economy, to give Canadians greater opportunities to invest and participate in the economic development of Canada.

The corporation

> concentrates on control-position equity in investments in leading corporations in selected industries. Industries characterized by large, longer-range development projects, an upgrading of Canadian resources, a high technological base, and a good potential for building a Canadian presence in international markets are considered. Six selected thus far are: petrochemicals, mining, oil and gas, health care, pipelines, and venture capital.[27]

The Canada Development Corporation can enter any industry, compete in any market, or buy out any firm it can persuade a majority of the stockholders to sell, without regard for the normal cannons of profitability. It is expected to be profitable, of course, but there is no enforcement of profitability, for, unlike a privately owned firm, it is not subject to the discipline of the capital market; its management cannot be replaced by dissatisfied stockholders, and it cannot itself be taken over if the market considers it less profitable than it might be. Nor is there a clear rule for deciding how to weigh profitability against such criteria as 'the upgrading of Canadian resources' or giving Canadians 'an opportunity to invest and participate in the economic development of Canada', should a conflict among criteria arise. In the absence of a rigid criterion of profitability, the Canada Development Corporation or its subsidiaries may be too harsh or too lenient with competitors, and there is no assurance that narrowly political criteria will not eventually come to influence its decisions.

Subsidization of investment, regulation of wages and prices, and public ownership of firms in industries predominantly in the private sector are part of a great armory of weapons that the government has gradually acquired to influence the profitability of the private sector, not just in the aggregate, or even at the industry level, but right down to the individual firm. There is a longstanding tradition of using government procurement as patronage. Regulation of firms to insure standards of work safety, product quality and care for the environment in the disposal of waste products has become an important determinant of the profitability of firms, yet the regulations themselves cannot always be framed so generally as to keep the profitability of particular firms independent of specific judgements as to whether and in what way a regulation applies to their behaviour. Anti-trust laws can be more or less rigidly enforced. And, above all, there is a wonderful assortment of weapons associated with foreign trade: tariffs can be specified precisely enough to refer to the output of a single, identifiable firm; anti-dumping duties can be imposed or removed at will; firms may be exempted from tariffs at the discretion of the responsible minister; and non-tariff barriers to trade (quotas and prohibitions) can be imposed without anyone, except possibly the domestic competitor, knowing what the tariff-equivalent of the impediment might be.[28]

Government intervention in the economy — crossing and sometimes effacing the line between public and private sectors — is not necessarily opposed by business, though, of course, some policies are less attractive than others. This may be due in part to an unwillingness of vulnerable firms to be seen actively opposing public policy, or to a judgement that it is more profitable to seek assistance for oneself than to object to its being granted to others. It may also arise from a belief that business in an interventionist economy need be no less profitable than business in an economy that is more intensely competitive. Firms, attuned to seek profit where profit is to be found, may be content with an environment where profit is in the gift of the government. Large firms may be especially adept at tapping profit from that source.

Of the weapons we have discussed, one would expect to see business supporting subsidization of investment, opposing public ownership of firms, and either supporting or opposing price and wage control depending upon which of the two is controlled the most; while those who favour the expansion of government might be expected to have the opposite preferences. It is interesting that, when each of these three weapons became an issue in Canadian elections, it was the socialist New Democratic Party that opposed subsidization of investment in 1972 as the giving of handouts to 'corporate welfare bums',[29] the ruling Liberal Party that opposed price and wage control in the election of 1974 (though, in fact, it introduced controls soon after the election), and the Conservative Party that campaigned vigorously and successfully on a platform of reprivatizing firms in the public sector in the election of 1979. The succession of events can be interpreted as signifying that the electorate has an instinctive understanding of the importance of equity and a willingness to support policies that contribute to its preservation, though the government of the day may be loudly reducing intervention in one respect while quietly extending it in another.

One would like to think that the new conservative trend in most Western countries represents a turning away from government intervention in the economy, and that it is no less antipathetic to the pro-business intervention of the traditional right as to the anti-business intervention of the traditional left. Capitalist equity requires that profitability of individual firms is not the gift of the government of the day and that firms be allowed to fail if they turn out to be unprofitable on their own. Capitalist equity requires a stance of government towards business that may, in practice, be less favourable to particular firms and less welcome to the business community than intervention. We have yet to see whether the new conservatism will differentiate in practice between the maintenance of capitalism as a form of industrial organization and the maintenance of the profitability of existing firms. We have yet to see whether the new conservatism can cultivate the indifference to the fate of particular firms that the capitalist system of equity, and the preservation of democratic government, requires.

In the course of this book it has been argued that democracy requires a system of equity; that the system need not be perfect as long as a substantial share of income is assigned outside and independently of the legislature; that the system of equity can at times be strengthened through redistribution of income; and that there are trends in most Western countries away from equity and towards greater political assignment of income — notably towards a greater share of government expenditure in the total national income, more goods and services provided directly by government rather than by the private sector, and progressively greater government influence upon the determination of income within the private sector. Economic policy can be designed to oppose these trends, but it is unlikely to do so unless equity is explicitly recognized as a criterion. When efficiency and equality are the only criteria, it may seem appropriate to impose a regulation here or a subsidy there, a tariff to favour an interest group that is particularly vocal at the moment, public participation in a nearly-bankrupt firm where workers are in danger of losing their jobs, greater influence of workers and civil servants upon decision-making in large firms, or wage and price control when inflation seems to be getting out of hand; for the long term cumulative effects of such measures are ignored. The economic foundation of democratic government may be allowed to erode gradually because we are not aware at each moment of the full consequences of our actions.

It is not at all clear where we stand now. The capitalist system of equity as it is today may still be strong enough for the continuance of democratic government. Democratic government may be viable for ever if we can freeze the economy in its present form with only minor adjustments to accommodate for technical change. But we cannot rule out the possibility that society is already in an unstable state, where democratic government works for the moment but cannot continue indefinitely unless the economy is reformed. It is at least arguable that the resurgence of regionalism and ethnic solidarity and the increasing tension in many countries between worker and management, rich and poor, despite the enormous improvement in the standard of living throughout this century, are symptoms of the increase in the share of income that the legislature has to assign.[30] In Canada, the deterioration of equity and the increasing dependence of each man's income upon negotiation with government and between federal and provincial governments may have contributed to the present situation, where conflict among regions is greater than ever before, and where English and French may be finding themselves unable to live within the same country.

What is clear is that a trend toward ever-greater political assignment of income must lead eventually to an economic organization that is no longer consistent with the continuance of democratic government. Englishmen, Canadians and Americans are too ready to suppose that democratic government is secure. With a 200-year history during which democratic government has never been threatened – during which neither military government nor the one-party state was a serious alternative – it is possible to believe democratic government to be inevitable, almost regardless of what we do, as though it were the reward for a special virtue that we possess and others do not. If this book convinces the reader of nothing else, I hope it succeeds in convincing him that democracy is not inevitable, that it rests on an economic foundation, and that it may be strengthened or destroyed altogether through the choice of economic policy.

Notes

PREFACE

(1)   Adam Smith, *The Wealth of Nations*, Cannan-Stigler edn, University of Chicago Press, 1976, pp. 494–5.

CHAPTER 1: INTRODUCTION

(1)   This quotation is a composite. The first part is from Harold J. Laski, *Democracy in Crisis*, Allen and Unwin, 1933, p. 215; the second part is a quotation from a pamphlet cited in Herbert A. Deane, *The Political Ideas of Harold J. Laski*, Columbia University Press, 1955, p. 195.
(2)   Friedrich A. Hayek, *The Road to Serfdom*, University of Chicago Press, 1944, p. 70. The quotation is preceded by a passage which comes close to summarizing the main theme of this book:

> It is the price of democracy that the possibilities of conscious control are restricted to the fields where true agreement exists and that in some fields things must be left to chance. But in a society which for its functioning depends on central planning, this control cannot be made dependent on a majority being able to agree: it will often be necessary that the will of a small minority be imposed upon the people, because this minority will be the largest group able to agree among themselves on the question at issue. Democratic government has worked successfully where, and so long as, the functions of government were by a widely-accepted creed, restricted to fields where agreement among a majority could be achieved by free discussion; and it is the great merit of the liberal creed that it reduced the range of subjects on which agreement was necessary to one which was likely to exist in a society of free men.

I do not mean to prejudge the issue. Whether the 'widely-accepted creed' has to be adherence to a capitalist form of economic organization, whether a mixed economy with elements of socialism and capitalism may not be more conducive to democracy than pure capitalism, whether there may not after all be some validity in Laski's remarks about capitalism and equality, are subjects to be discussed in this book.
(3)   Joseph A. Schumpeter, *Capitalism, Socialism and Democracy*, 2nd edn, Harper, 1942, p. 284.
(4)   The impetus for the study of political implications of economic policy since the Second World War has come predominantly, though not entirely, from game theory, a mode of analysis encompassing a wider range of activity and a more direct representation of social conflict than is allowed for in traditional economics. The

classic is John von Neumann and Oskar Morgenstern, *The Theory of Games and Economic Activity*, Princeton University Press, 1947. Duncan Black's *The Theory of Committees and Elections*, Cambridge University Press, 1958, and Kenneth Arrow's *Social Choice and Individual Values*, John Wiley, 1951, have also been very influential in provoking economists to look more closely at politics and in providing a theory and a language in which economic concepts can be brought to bear. In writing this book, I have been influenced by the writings of James Buchanan and Gordon Tullock — especially *The Calculus of Consent: Legal Foundations of Constitutional Democracy*, University of Michigan Press, 1962. I must emphasize my debt to Buchanan and Tullock because, while I have quietly borrowed many of their ideas, I disagree with them on certain matters and the points of disagreement are discussed in this book.

(5)   By the economic model, I mean the model of the competitive economy as set out simply and intuitively in elementary texts such as Paul A. Samuelson's *Economics*, 9th edn, McGraw-Hill, 1973, and analysed rigorously in works on general equilibrium such as Kenneth J. Arrow and F.H. Hahn, *General Competitive Analysis*, Holden Day, 1971.

(6)   Frank H. Knight, 'The Ethics of Competition', an essay included in Knight's *The Ethics of Competition and Other Essays*, Harper, 1935. The word 'ethics' in the title has a double meaning. It refers at once to the ethical worth of competition as an institution and the ethics that competition tends to foster. The ethics (in the latter sense) of communism is a favourite subject of Alexander Solzhenitsyn. The theme runs through all his novels, especially *Cancer Ward*, where the hospital is a display case of communist personality types. The standard of morality fostered by a collectivist organization of society — as distinct from the justification of that society — is beautifully analysed in Hayek's *The Road to Serfdom* in the chapter entitled 'Why the Worst get on Top'.

(7)   The distinction between the individualistic and collectivist premises is discussed in James M. Buchanan and Gordon Tullock, *The Calculus of Consent*, University of Michigan Press, 1962.

CHAPTER 2: HOW A SYSTEM OF EQUITY ENABLES SOCIETY TO COPE WITH THE INSTABILITY OF DEMOCRACY

(1)   James Madison, *The Federalist*, edited by B.F. Wright, Harvard University Press, 1961, pp. 32 and 33.

(2)   This example is well known to game theorists. See, for instance, Duncan Luce and Howard Raiffa, *Games and Decisions*, 1952, Chapter 13. Its political implications are analysed in some detail in Gordon Tullock, 'Problems of Majority Voting', *The Journal of Political Economy*, 1959, pp. 571–9, and in James M. Buchanan and Gordon Tullock, *The Calculus of Consent: Legal Foundations of Constitutional Democracy*, University of Michigan Press, 1962.

(3)   How associations of rats originate, how rats distinguish between members of an association and outsiders, and how behaviour of rats to one another differs according to whether they are members of the same association, is described in Konrad Lorenz, *On Aggression*, Chapter 10, Methuen, 1966.

(4)   In the language of game theory, we may say that majority rule is a game without a core.

(5)   Writing, let it be remembered, in 1776, Adam Smith argued that the American colonists would be better off in a union with Great Britain than they would be as an independent nation because union

would, at least, deliver them from those rancorous and virulent factions which are inseparable from small democracies, and which have so frequently divided the affections of their people, and disturbed the tranquility of their govern-ments, in their form so nearly democratical. In the case of a total separation from Great Britain, which, unless prevented by a union of this kind, seems very likely to take place, those factions would be ten times more virulent than ever. Before the commencement of the present disturbances, the coercive power of the mother-country had always been able to restrain those factions from breaking out into anything worse than gross brutality and insult. If that coercive power were entirely taken away, they would probably soon break out into open violence and bloodshed. In all great countries which are united under one uniform government, the spirit of party commonly prevails less in the remote provinces than in the centre of the empire. The distance of those provinces from the capital, from the principal seat of the great scramble of faction and ambition, makes them enter less into the view of any of the con-tending parties, and renders them more indifferent and impartial spectators of the conduct of all. Adam Smith, *The Wealth of Nations*, Cannan-Stigler edn, University of Chicago Press, 1976, p. 484.

(6)   For a two-man economy, the degree of feasibility may be defined with the aid of a diagram, in which the vertical axis represents the income of Mr 1, the horizontal

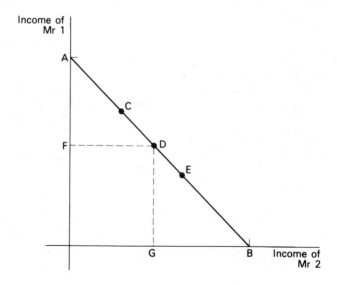

axis represents the income of Mr 2, and the line AB, at 45° to both axes, shows all possible assignments to Mr 1 and Mr 2 of total national income, represented by the equal distances OA and OB. For instance, at the point D, the income of Mr 1 is OF and the income of Mr 2 is OG; at A, the whole of the national income accrues to Mr 1; at B, the whole national income accrues to Mr 2. If there is a prior agreement that, regardless of what the legislature decides, the income of Mr 1 cannot fall below the amount corresponding to the point E while the income of Mr 2 cannot fall below the amount corresponding to the point C, then the degree of feasibility is one minus the ratio of CE to AB expressed as a percentage. The degree of feasibility is 100% if there is a prior agreement that the assignment of incomes to Mr 1 and Mr 2 will correspond to some particular point such as D. The degree of feasibility would also be 100% if there were agreement on a mechanism that might generate any of a number of assignments on the line, as long as the particular assignment were determined by the mechanism alone, and not by the legislature.

(7)   Views of a number of leading political theorists on the role of consensus in democracy are discussed and analysed in Elias Berg, *Democracy and the Majority Principle*, Scandinavian University Books, 1965. In *A Preface to Democratic Theory*, University of Chicago Press, 1956, p. 132, Robert A. Dahl writes:

> What we ordinarily describe as democratic politics is merely the chaff. It is the surface manifestation, representing superficial conflicts. Prior to politics, beneath it, enveloping it, is the underlying consensus on policy that usually exists in society among a predominant portion of the politically active members. Without such a consensus, no democratic system would long survive the endless irritations and frustrations of elections and party competition. With such a consensus, the disputes over policy alternatives are nearly always disputes over a set of alternatives that have already been winnowed to those within a broad area of basic agreement.

It is an unfortunate consequence of the separation of economics and politics as academic subjects that the notion of consensus as a prerequisite to democracy has not, until recently, been extended to the study of economic organization.

(8)   See Ernest Barker (ed.), *The Politics of Aristotle*, Oxford University Press, 1958, Appendix 2.

(9)   Richard Musgrave, *The Theory of Public Finance*, McGraw-Hill, 1959, pp. 160–82.

CHAPTER 3: EXTENSION TO A COMPLEX SOCIETY

(1)   Adam Smith, *The Wealth of Nations*, Cannan-Stigler eds., University of Chicago Press, 1976, p. 477.

(2)   Kenneth J. Arrow and F.H. Hahn, *General Competitive Analysis*, Holden-Day and Oliver and Boyd, 1971, pp. vi–vii.

(3)   The concept of single-peaked issues is due to Duncan Black, and is carefully analysed in his *The Theory of Committees and Elections*, Cambridge University Press, 1958.

(4)   The implications of the paradox of voting for social choice is the subject of Kenneth J. Arrow, *Social Choice and Individual Values*, John Wiley, 1951. Voting by majority rule is not the only means of social choice that gives rise to inconsistencies. It is proved that, subject to certain intuitively reasonable conditions, there can exist no rule by which individual rankings can be consistently transformed into a social ranking.

(5)   This issue has been studied extensively under the heading of 'optimal taxation'. It is assumed that people differ in skill and that the national income is affected adversely by taxation through its impact on the supply of labour, the propensity to save or the propensity to educate oneself. The conditions under which the progressivity of the tax system is single-peaked have been specified and optimal schedules of tax rates computed on various assumptions about the form of the utility function and the constraints in the economy. See particularly Anthony B. Atkinson, 'How Progressive should the Income Tax Be?' in Edmund S. Phelps (ed.), *Economic Justice*, Penguin, 1974.

(6)   Views differ on whether logrolling improves or worsens the outcome of government by majority rule. James Buchanan and Gordon Tullock see logrolling as a means of 'squeezing out allocational inefficiencies' in government by majority rule (*The Calculus of Consent*, University of Michigan Press, 1962, p. 198). Brams, on the other hand, sees it as a means by which issues that are single-peaked individually may be factional in combination. See Steven J. Brams, *Game Theory and Politics*, Free Press, 1975, pp. 129–31.

(7)   The proofs of these assertions, and the exact specification of the conditions under which they are true, are contained in Arrow and Hahn, *General Competitive Analysis*. There are two principal theorems in welfare economics: (a) that there exists a set of prices at which there is no excess demand for any good when all firms maximize profits and all consumers deploy their resources and spend their income to maximize their individual welfare, and (b) that the equilibrium is Pareto-optimal, by which is meant that no change in the allocation of goods and services can make everyone better off. It is the first of these propositions that is important from our point of view because there is nothing comparable to a competitive equilibrium in assignment by voting with majority rule.

(8)   The social and political consequences of public assignment of an indispensable means of production are analysed in Karl A. Wittfogel, *Oriental Despotism: A Comparative Study of Total Power*, Yale University Press, 1957. Wittfogel developed the thesis, of which the germ is to be found in the writing of Karl Marx, that the despotism of the great empires in China and the Near East rested on the control of vast systems of irrigation. Empires came into being and were preserved because the allocation of water among farms could be attended to in no other way.

(9)   See Samuel Brittan and Barry Riley, 'A People's Stake in North Sea Oil', *Lloyds Bank Review*, April 1978.

(10)   In Robert J. Aumann and Mordecai Kurtz, 'Power and Taxes', *Econometrica*, July 1977, pp. 1137–61, it is shown that there exists an equilibrium system of tax and redistribution when decisions are arrived at by majority rule and each agent can destroy part of his endowment, the equivalent in that model of a strike; the proof of existence seems to depend on a behavioural assumption equivalent to supposing that each person is assigned income more or less in proportion to his capacity and willingness to destroy resources if his income is inadequate.

(11)   Milovan Djilas, *The New Class: An Analysis of the Communist System*, Praeger, 1957.

(12)   But see William A. Niskanen, Jr, *Bureaucracy and Representative Government*, Aldine-Atherton, 1971, and Ludwig von Mises, *Bureaucracy*, Yale University Press, 1944.

(13)   M. I. Finley, *Democracy Ancient and Modern*, Rutgers University Press, 1972, p. 25.

(14)   The story of the emergence of English Parliament in the Middle Ages and its defence against the King's servants in the Renaissance is told in Norman F. Cantor, *The English*, Simon and Schuster, 1968.

(15)   The inherent instability and eventual destruction of democracy in several plural societies is analysed in Alvin Rabushka and Kenneth A. Shepsle, *Politics of Plural Societies: A Theory of Democratic Instability*, Charles E. Merrill, 1972. Rabushka and Shepsle note with approval Furnival's view (S.J. Furnival, *Netherlands India*, Cambridge University Press, 1939) that a plural society requires an external force, such as a colonial administration, to hold it together. Aristotle has this to say: 'A state cannot be constituted from any chance body of persons, or in any chance period of time. Most of the states that have admitted members of another stock, either at the time of their foundation or later, have been troubled by sedition.' (Ernest Barker (ed.), *The Politics of Aristotle*, Oxford University Press, 1958, p. 210.)

(16)   'the leaders of a Parent-Teacher Association must take some account of the fact that their proposals must be acceptable to members who also belong to the local taxpayers' league, to the local Chamber of Commerce, and to the Catholic Church.' This passage is from David B. Truman, *The Governmental Process*, Knopf, 1951, p. 509. The concept is analysed in Douglas W. Rae and Michael Taylor, *The Analysis of Political Cleavages*, Yale University Press, 1970.

(17)

> Democrats 'say' that justice consists in the will of the majority of persons. Oligarchs 'say' that it consists in the will of a majority of property owners and that decisions should be taken on the basis of weight of property. Both these answers involve inequality and injustice . . . if we carry the oligarchical conception of justice to its logical consequence, a single person who owns more than all other owners of property put together will have a just claim to be the sole ruler. If, on the other hand, justice is made to consist of the will of the majority of persons, that majority will be seen to act unjustly . . . and to confiscate the property of the rich minority.'

Aristotle goes on to say that 'we may attribute sovereignty to the will of a majority of persons who are also owners of a majority of property'. He gives an example of how this would work out in practice; I find the example confusing (*The Politics of Aristotle*, pp. 260–1).

(18)   On their way to chop off the head of King Charles, Cromwell's army stopped at a place called Putney to debate the principles of political philosophy, for they had no experience of and no precedent for governing without a king. The most pressing issue was the extent of the franchise in the new Parliament. Two main views were expressed. Some felt that universal franchise would be appropriate because in the absence of a king each Englishman should have the same influence on government as every other and because the soldiers who fought for the overthrow of the Stuarts

but who, for the most part, had incomes below what was proposed as the minimum to entitle one to the vote ought not, on that account, be denied a stake in the new government. Cromwell himself, supported by his son-in-law Henry Ireton, held a different view. They favoured property qualifications for the sorts of reasons discussed in the text, namely that property is indispensable for the maintenance of civilised society and that the institution of property can be preserved only if the poor are somehow prevented from voting it out of existence. In the words of Henry Ireton:

> that a man should have the power of choosing those men that shall determine what shall be the law in this state, though he himself has no permanent interest in the state [by which Ireton appears to mean 'no property'] . . . if this be allowed [because by the right of nature] we are free, we are equal, one man must have as much voice as another, then show me what step or difference [there is], why [I may not] by the same right [take your property]. . . . If you do hold up this law of nature, I would fair have any man show men their bounds where you will end, and [why you should not] take away all property.

The whole debate is reproduced in A.S.P. Woodhouse, *Puritanism and Liberty; being the Army Debates 1647–49*, 2nd edn, University of Chicago Press, 1974. The quotation is from page 48, and the words in brackets are inserted where the editor felt that they were missing from the text.

(19) The matter is discussed in 'The Politics of the Classical Economics' (*Quarterly Journal of Economics*, 1948, pp. 714–47) by W.D. Grampp, whose description of the problem of majority rule is worth quoting at some length:

> In urging economic freedom upon the world, the classicists were . . . insisting that all men should have the right to seek their material welfare in their own way . . . . Yet in their observations on political doctrine and organization of the state (as distinct from organization of the market) they were far from holding democratic views, and although they favoured a representative government, they quite pointedly wished it to be a limited one. In the opposition of these views is a paradox: a free market implies what may be called universal economic enfranchisement, but limitations on representative government deny even the political freedom which is the analogue of a free market. [p. 714]

> In order that the behaviour of each person promote the welfare of others as well as of himself, it was necessary (the economists believed) to accord representation to those who had a private interest in keeping the peace and to withhold it from those who did not. It is to the interest of those with property to support government, as a law enforcing agency, and so they are included in suffrage; but the propertyless have no interest in law and peace and so (the economists believed) should be excluded. The limitation was not imposed because it was thought that the poor were desperately covetous. Everyone was thought to be naturally avaricious. But men of property could be more depended upon to restrain their cupidity: first, because, having a private interest to be protected, they were more aware of the general interest served by governments; and, second, because they wished to secure this private interest

even though such security forced them to sacrifice the possibility of a larger gain (because, presumably, they favoured a certain smaller sum than an uncertain large one). The propertyless, however, had nothing to lose, and, when matters came to a certain point of desperation, they conceivably would seek their interest in gambling on a political upheaval on the chance of acquiring some fortune. In a less extreme case, they might seek to improve their position by legislation that discriminated against wealth . . . . Stated in summary fashion, the psychology of the classical economists dictated the exclusion of the poor from the franchise, because the natural covetousness of the poor would bring social disorder if allowed to express itself politically. [p. 731]

It must be observed that this idea of limited representation was in no way a justification of aristocracy and monarchy. That rationalization runs in a quite different direction and follows from an assumption that there is an elite class which by reason of its superior talents and exclusive political wisdom necessarily should be given power. If the economists entertained such ideas, they were most reluctant to express them . . . they ascribed the same motives to the upper classes as to the lower. [p. 740]

CHAPTER 4: EQUALITY AND SOCIALISM

(1)   Ludwig von Mises, *Socialism*, Jonathan Cape, 1936, p. 85.
(2)   Oskar Lange, 'On the Economic Theory of Socialism', in B.E. Lippincott (ed.), *On the Economic Theory of Socialism*, McGraw-Hill, 1938, p. 109.
(3)   The maximin principle is the doctrine that our notions of what is just and unjust can be rationalized with reference to the worst off person in society. On this principle, a change in laws or institutions is just if the condition of the worst off man in the new circumstances is better than the condition of the worst off man (a different person in each case) in the original circumstances. A planning commission following the maximin principle adopts a lexigraphic criterion in its ranking of all possible states of the economy. It first chooses the state or states with the highest income for the worst off person. If there is only one such state, that state is chosen. If there are several, the planner chooses among them in accordance with the welfare of the next worst off person. And so on, until a unique state emerges. My opinion of this procedure is that it is preposterous both as a model of judgement of what is just and what is not, and as a criterion for a planner to follow. Taken literally, it means that a slight deterioration in the condition of the worst off person is considered more important than a major improvement in the well-being of millions of other people who may at the outset have been no better off than the worst off person. Otherwise, if the principle is treated as a vague expression of concern for the poor, it becomes indistinguishable from classical utilitarianism. The principle is put forward in detail in John Rawls, *A Theory of Justice*, Harvard University Press, 1971, a book well worth reading despite this difficulty for its grounding of the principles of justice in a social contract considered as a device for deriving judgements of what is best for society from judgements of what is best for oneself by imagining oneself as a randomly-selected person in each of the options compared.

(4)   Marx himself was reluctant to describe the economy that would emerge once capitalism was overthrown. Bourgeois economists showed no such inhibitions, being only too pleased to reciprocate for socialist theorists' analysis of capitalism; and the socialists eventually felt compelled to respond. Key articles by Pierson (1902), von Mises (1920), Halm (1935) and Hayek (1935), arguing that output is considerably lower in a centrally-planned, socialist economy than in a competitive economy, and by Barone (1908), Taylor (1929) and Lange (1937), arguing the opposite case, are to be found in B.E. Lippincott (ed.), *On the Economic Theory of Socialism,* McGraw-Hill, 1938 (which contains the pieces by Taylor and Lange) and F.A. Hayek (ed.), *Collectivist Economic Planning,* Routledge & Kegan Paul, 1935 (which contains the rest). Ludwig von Mises, *Socialism,* Jonathan Cape, 1936 (translated from the original German edition of 1922 by J. Kahane) is somewhat melodramatic but great fun and very perceptive.

CHAPTER 5: CAPITALISM AS A SYSTEM OF EQUITY

(1)   Ludwig von Mises, *Socialism*, Yale University Press, 1951, p. 43.

(2)   For a different view see, Joan Robinson, *The Economics of Imperfect Competition,* Macmillan, 1933, Chapter 27, entitled 'A World of Monopolies'.

(3)   For a rigorous but none the less simple exposition of bilateral monopoly, see P.J. Newman, *The Theory of Exchange,* Prentice-Hall, 1965, especially Chapter 3.

(4)   In 1978, some American steel companies announced price increases on all grades of steel produced in the United States. President Carter then threatened to lower tariffs on the import of steel as a means of forcing domestic firms to lower prices again. A spokesman of the steel industry was quoted as saying '. . . we'll go offshore. There are a lot of places where they would love to have our money and get some jobs. And then we'll sell to the US market' (Fortune, 8 May 1978, p. 47).

(5)   On 2 August 1971 the Senate passed a bill guaranteeing loans of up to $250 million by the Lockhead Corporation, saving the corporation from probable bankruptcy and preventing its 60,000 employees from losing their jobs. But in 1971, out of a total of about two and a half million firms, 10.3 thousand firms with average liabilities of $186,000 were allowed to fail without protest from Congress even though the total number of jobs lost was probably in the order of a million, twenty odd times the number of jobs that would have been lost if Lockhead had failed and if no part of the firm had been reorganized to operate on its own. The big firm was preserved because it was visible and concentrated in its impact on the economy. The small firms were allowed to fail because they could not combine to exert pressure collectively. See 'Senate votes Lockhead Aid', *Wall Street Journal,* 3 August 1971, p. 2, and *Statistical abstract of the United States,* 1977, Tables 935 and 906. The number of jobs lost through bankruptcy was estimated from data on the number and liabilities of bankrupt firms by supposing that there was a job lost for every $20,000 liabilities, a figure roughly consistent with evidence of assets per man employed in the US corporations.

(6)   This issue is discussed in connection with co-determination and the corporate state in Chapter 6.

(7)   In his study of the share of the 100 largest firms in Britain, S.J. Prais found that virtually no part of the substantial increase over this century could be attributed to an increase in plant size. The share of the 100 largest *establishments* has remained virtually constant despite the rise in the share of the 100 largest enterprises. The growth in the 100 largest enterprises would seem to be entirely due to an increase in the number of establishments per firm. In fact, the average size of establishment in the 100 largest enterprises actually fell from 750 men in 1958 to 430 men in 1972. It follows, therefore, that such economies of scale as there may be are not at the level of the establishment at all, but are associated with finance, advertising, research or other factors affecting the enterprises as a whole. See S.J. Prais, *The Evolution of Giant Firms in Britain*, Cambridge University Press, 1976, Chapters 3 and 4.

(8)   See Warren G. Nutter and Henry A. Einhorn, *Enterprise Monopoly in the United States 1899–1958*, Columbia University Press, 1969.

(9)   Government expenditure as a share of gross domestic product has been growing in all of the OECD countries. The record from 1962 to 1975 is summarized in *Public Expenditure Trends, OECD,* June 1978.

(10)   Not entirely. The defence of capitalism is the defence of privilege in the sense that people with property or large incomes can consume more than people without these advantages. But capitalism is the enemy of privilege in the sense that it has no respect for established wealth. Old firms are frequently destroyed by smaller and more vigorous rivals. Established interests will often try to constrain the market and to modify the institutions of capitalism by restricting entry to lucrative lines of business as a means of preserving their own income and status.

(11)   Morton Paglin, 'Transfers in Kind: Their Impact on Poverty', a paper presented for the Hoover Institution Conference on Income Redistribution, 1977.

(12)   The typical pattern of earnings over a person's life cycle is that his earnings are low when he is young, rise to a peak in middle age, and fall with age afterwards. What seems to be happening is that the life cycle of earnings is becoming more pronounced as time goes on, leading to greater variability in a given person's earnings over the years of his life. The effect of this change upon a cross-section of the earnings of different people is to make the distribution of earnings seem more unequal even if the distribution of lifetime incomes remains neither more nor less unequal than it was before. See Morton Paglin, 'The Measurement of the Trend on Inequality: a basic Revision', *American Economic Review*, 1975, pp. 598–609.

(13)   There may be a sort of homeostasis in the distribution of income. In the 1960s many programmes were established to transfer income to the poor, and taxes had to be increased to finance these programmes. Any tendency for taxes to be shifted forward would disequalize the pretax distribution of income though the after-tax incomes may be equalized considerably. See Edgar K. Browning, 'The Trend toward Equality in the Distribution of Net Income', *Southern Economic Journal*, 1974, pp. 912–22.

(14)   James D. Smith and Stephen D. Franklin, 'The Concentration of Personal Wealth, 1922–1969', *American Economic Review, Papers and Proceedings*, 1974, pp. 162–7.

(15)   On Wolsey's income, see A.F. Pollard, *Wolsey*, Longman, Green, 1927, p. 321. Wolsey's income was estimated at £35,000 a year for the year 1531. The wages rate of £6 a year for that year is estimated from data in E.H. Phelps Brown and Sheila

V. Hopkins, 'Seven Centuries of Building Wages', *Economica*, 1955, pp.195–206. They state the wage for that year to be 4d. per day for a labourer and 6d. per day for a craftsman in the building trade. The average of 5d. per day comes to £6 per year if it is supposed that an average man works 300 days a year.

(16)   Average family income in the United States in 1976 was about $15,000. *Statistical Abstract of the United States*, 1977, Table 714.

(17)   Lee Soltow, 'Long-run Changes in British Income Inequality', *Economic History Review*, 1968, pp. 17–29.

(18)   Some years ago, when I was living in England, my daughter noticed the royal coat of arms and the statement 'Provisioner of Cereals to Her Majesty the Queen' on a box of corn flakes. 'Does the Queen eat corn flakes?' she asked; for brought up on fairy tales she found it difficult to believe that the Queen might eat the same breakfast food as herself. In fact, it is only in recent times that rich and poor have eaten more or less the same food, and diets differ more from one person to the next through preference than from differences in wealth. It is still possible, in parts of England and among people of the older generation to identify a man's social class by his height. You cannot make such an identification among people born since the Second World War.

CHAPTER 6: THE POLITICAL IMPLICATIONS OF ECONOMIC POLICY

(1)   Ernest Barker (ed.), *The Politics of Aristotle*, Oxford University Press, 1958, p. 269.

(2)   See, for instance, Arthur M. Okun, *Equality and Efficiency: The Big Tradeoff*, Brookings Institution, 1974. Actually, Okun's stance on economic policy is closer to mine than the title suggests because he is very much concerned with equality of rights and not just with equality of income.

(3)   Henry C. Simons, *Personal Income Taxation*, University of Chicago Press, 1938, p.50.

(4)   Meyer Bucovetsky and Richard M. Bird, 'Tax Reform in Canada: a Progress Report', *National Tax Journal*. 1972, pp. 15–41

(5)   A.B. Atkinson and J.E. Stiglitz, 'The Design of Tax Structure: Direct versus Indirect Taxation', *Journal of Public Economics*, 1976, pp. 55–75.

(6)   Henry Simons states, in *Personal Income Taxation*, that

income must be conceived as something quantitative and objective. It must be reasonable; indeed, definition must indicate or clearly imply an actual procedure of measuring. Moreover, the arbitrary distinction implicit in one's definition must be reduced to a minimum. [pp. 42–3]

and

Administrators may not concern themselves greatly about considerations of justice; but they should be vitally concerned as to whether levies like the income tax are generally felt to be clearly inequitable. [Notice that Simons is using the term 'equity' in exactly the sence of this book.] This feeling, we venture, is more likely to arise where persons are seen to pay very different taxes for no good reason, or to pay similarly when difference is clearly appropriate, than where the general level of rates or degree of progression is high for all alike. Thus, avoidance of obvious and flagrant inequity is imperative . . . [pp. 108–9]

Pros and cons of the comprehensive tax base are discussed in B.I. Bittker, C.O. Galvin, R.A. Musgrave and J.A. Peckman, *A Comprehensive Income Tax Base: A Debate*, Federal Tax Press, 1968.

(7) For an example of such a scheme, see Vernon L. Smith, 'The Principle of Unanimity and Voluntrary Consent in Social Choice', *Journal of Political Economy*, 1977, pp. 1125–39.

(8) For a spirited defence of the 'efficiency only' position, see Robert H. Bork, *The Anti-trust Paradox, a Policy at War with Itself*, Basic Books, 1978.

(9) Quoted in Bork, *Anti-trust Paradox*, (p. 25). Bork considers this statement as an aberration, a lapse from what is otherwise a consistent determination on Justice Peckham's part to assess business practices by their effects on efficiency alone.

(10) Carl Kaysen and Donald F. Turner, *Anti-trust Policy: an Economic and Legal Analysis*, Harvard University Press, 1965, pp. 17–18.

(11) The progressive corporation income tax has been recommended by S.J. Prais, *The Evolution of Giant Firms in Britain*, Cambridge University Press, 1976, Chapter 7.

(12)

In political discussion . . . scholars seem to have overlooked the central place that the unanimity rule must occupy in any normative theory of democratic government. We have witnessed an inversion whereby majority rule has been elevated to the status which the unanimity rule should occupy. At best, majority rule should be viewed as one among many practical expedients . . . [James Buchanan and Gordon Tullock, *The Calculus of Consent*, University of Michigan Press, 1962, p. 96]

Introduced into the literature of economics by Knut Wicksell ('A Principle of Just Taxation', reprinted in Richard A. Musgrave and Alan T. Peacock (eds.) *Classics in the Theory of Public Finance*, Macmillan, 1958), the unanimity principle has been rediscovered and vigorously advocated by James Buchanan and has become the basis of a new and increasingly important approach to public finance, in which society is looked upon as a contract that ought not to be revised without the consent of all parties concerned.

(13) See A.K. Sen, *On Economic Inequality*, Clarendon Press, 1973, pp. 96–9. An economy where everyone would be content to work hard voluntarily as long as most others did so too is characterized by two stable equilibria — a diligent equilibrium, where everyone works hard because everyone else works hard, and a shirkers' equilibrium, where no one works hard because no one else works hard. A law requiring everyone to work hard may therefore be necessary despite the fact that no one has any inclination to violate the law; this is an instance of the assurance paradox. A comparable situation can arise in political life. There may be need of a constitutional provision to forbid any majority from passing a certain type of law despite the fact

The effect of transfers on
the distribution of family income
in the United States, 1976
($billions)

Quintile	Pre-tax pre-transfer income	Social insurance added	Cash transfers added	In-kind transfers added	Post-tax/ post-transfer income
Low 20%	3.3	42.9	54.0	75.8	75.1
Second 20%	76.3	111.5	115.2	126.0	119.7
Third 20%	173.7	193.8	195.5	199.8	172.6
Fourth 20%	276.1	291.0	291.9	294.1	243.7
High 20%	534.1	548.4	549.1	550.9	429.7
Total[a]	$1,063.4	$1,187.4	$1,205.4	$1,246.4	$1,040.3

Source: Poverty Status of Families under Alternative Definitions of Income, Background Paper No. 17 (13 January 1977), Congressional Budget Office, Congress of the United States.

that no majority would ever want to pass such a law as long as it is confident that the constitution will hold.

(14) The combined effect of transfers — including social security, cash transfers such as direct welfare payment to the very poor, and in-kind transfers such as food stamps — on the poorest 20% of the population of the United States was to raise their total income in 1976 from $3.3 billion to $75.1 billion. The effect of transfers on the distribution as a whole is shown in the accompanying table.

(15) The Economy of Love and Fear is the title of a book by Kenneth E. Boulding, Wadsworth Publishing Company, 1973.

(16) The argument is that the transfer is a genuine cost to the donor but a spurious gain to the recipient. The immediate donor may be the government but the ultimate donor is, of course, the taxpayer, who must finance the expenditure. The gain is spurious because people, knowing there are gains to be had, compete for political influence until the cost of competing just equals the value of the chance of getting the grant. This argument was first put forward by Gordon Tullock in 'The Cost of Transfers', Kyklos, 1971, pp. 629—43. See also the discussion on this point between Tullock and Edgar K. Browning in Kyklos, 1972, pp. 374—81. The social implications of this argument are developed in Ann O. Krueger, 'The Political Economy of Rent-seeking Society', American Economic Review, 1974, pp. 291—303.

(17) For a description of the American transfer system, see Barry R. Chiswick, 'The Income Transfer System: Impact, Viability, and Proposals for Reform', in W. Fellner (ed.), Contemporary Economic Problems 1977, American Enterprise Institute, 1978.

(18) It can be proved on simple but not altogether unreasonable assumptions that a community is more likely to vote for the socialization of a commodity — that is, a higher proportion will favour socialization other things being equal — the more unequal is the initial distribution of income. Equalization of the distribution of income is, therefore, a way of forestalling socialization. I have examined these ques-

tions in 'The Welfare Economics of the Socialization of Commodities', *Journal of Public Economics*, 1977, pp. 151–68.

(19)   'Why they are Starving in West Bengal', *The Economist*, 26 October, 1974. Another similar example was reported in the *Wall Street Journal* on 28 April 1979. A tidal wave had struck several villages on the Bay of Bengal. As a result, the soil was clogged with sea-salt and had to be washed with fresh water before crops could be grown again. The government delayed for weeks making the announcement that water would be made available until an opportune moment could be found for telling farmers in areas not affected by the disaster that their water allotments would be correspondingly reduced. The point is that, as the government controlled the water supply, political pressure had to be an important determinant of who would get the water. Socialization is often divisive in a society not rich enough to provide as much of the socialized commodity as anybody wants to use.

(20)   The overall supply curve of doctors may be upward-sloping, but the elasticity of supply to the government is nearly infinite because the government does not hire a large enough proportion of the whole stock of doctors to affect the wage significantly.

(21)   By the high-tax coalition, I mean those groups that have a special incentive to encourage high taxes and high government expenditure not just because they want the type of goods the public sector may provide, but because they are special beneficiaries as employees or as recipients of transfers of public expenditure. Obviously, the high-tax coalition is not a well defined concept, and any attempt to identify it has to be impressionistic at best. I would be inclined to identify three categories of people as special beneficiaries of public expenditure: the lowest quintile of the income distribution, much of whose income takes the form of transfers; the old; and government employees. The first group constitutes 20% of the population by definition. The old constitute another 14.8% of all families, but of these 42% have incomes in the lowest quintile, leaving 8.6% of the families that are old but not in the first group. Public employees, presumed to be neither old nor in the lowest quintile, constitute 15 million workers out of a civilian labour force of 92.6 million, or 16.2%. We shall suppose this percentage to represent the voting strength of civil servants and their dependents. The size of the coalition as a percentage of the electorate is estimated to be:

	%
The poor	20
The old	8.6
The public employees	16.2
Total	44.8

All figures are for the year 1975 and are taken from the *Statistical Abstract of the United States 1975* and Current Population Reports, Series P–60, No. 105, Bureau of the Census, US Department of Commerce.

The reader is warned once again that the notion of a high-tax coalition is necessarily vague, that the estimate of its membership is as crude as any estimate can be, and that people identified here as members of the high-tax coalition may vote to reduce government spending. The identification of a special incentive to vote for increased spending does not imply that the special interest will take precedence over the interest shared with the rest of the population, in keeping spending down.

(22) J.E. Cloutier, 'The Distribution of Benefits and Costs of Social Security in Canada, 1971–1975', Discussion Paper No. 108, Economic Council of Canada. The very poorest quintile gets little from unemployment insurance while the remaining quantiles share more or less equally. The culprits are the working wives with weak attachment to the labour force, who draw unemployment insurance though they are not really looking for work. Such behaviour is more frequently to be observed in families where the husband's earnings are sufficient to maintain the family whether the wife works or not. Actually, the overall effect of unemployment insurance is redistributive in Canada if the tax costs as well as the benefits of the scheme are taken into account.

(23) W.M. Corden, *Trade Policy and Economic Welfare*, Clarendon Press, 1974.

(24) These programmes are described in *ABC: Assistance to Business in Canada*, Board of Economic Development Ministers, Government of Canada, 1979; the passages in quotations are from this source.

(25) *Canada Yearbook*, 1977, p. 1055.

(26) Lists of public sector firms under federal and provincial jurisdiction are to be found in *Minutes and Proceedings and Evidence of the Standing Committee on Public Accounts*, House of Commons, 17 May 1977, and *Provincial Government Enterprise Finance*, Statistics Canada, 61–204, published annually.

(27) *Canada Yearbook, 1977*, p. 1039. It should be added that there is provision for private as well as government participation in the Canada Development Corporation. At present, the federal government is the majority shareholder but it need not remain so.

(28) Klaus Stegemann, *Canadian Non-Tariff Barriers to Trade*, Private Planning Association, 1973.

(29) David Lewis, *Louder Voices: The Corporate Welfare Bums*, James Lewis & Samuel, 1972.

Index